SEA KAYAK
STROKES

SEA KAYAK
STROKES

A GUIDE TO EFFICIENT PADDLING SKILLS

DOUG ALDERSON

Rocky
Mountain Books

VANCOUVER · VICTORIA · CALGARY

Rocky Mountain Books
#108 – 17665 66A Avenue
Surrey, BC V3S 2A7
www.rmbooks.com

Rocky Mountain Books
PO Box 468
Custer, WA
98240-0468

LIBRARY AND ARCHIVES CANADA CATALOGUING IN PUBLICATION
Alderson, Doug
Sea kayak strokes : a guide to efficient paddling skills / Doug Alderson.
ISBN 978-1-894765-85-5
1.   Sea kayaking. I. Title.
2.   GV788.5.A42 2007   797.122'4   C2006-906600-0

LIBRARY OF CONGRESS CONTROL NUMBER: 2006940310

Edited by Corina Skavberg
Cover and interior design by Jacqui Thomas
Front cover photo Doug Alderson
Interior photos and drawings by Doug Alderson

Printed in Canada

Rocky Mountain Books acknowledges the financial support for its publishing program from the Government of Canada through the Book Publishing Industry Development Program (BPIDP).

CONTENTS

ACKNOWLEDGEMENTS

Many paddlers from across Canada offered their time, paddling about in circles and bracing just one more, and another one more time. Their contribution of time and paddling skill is central to this book. My sincere thanks and appreciation go out to these paddlers who were brave enough to paddle in front of the camera. As they appear in order: Karen Dominick, Michael Pardy, Richard Alexander, David Wells, Glynis Newman, Jen Smith, Andrew Woodford, Nic Castro, James Vasilyev, Ian Doherty, Nancy Doherty, James Roberts, Ian (Roscoe) Ross and Thomas Alderson. Further thanks go out to the greater number of paddlers who came out to support me in this project. Many of these paddlers are instructors and coaches who spend significant portions of their leisure time passing along their skillful technique and love of the outdoors to old and new friends alike. Wherever I have been invited to paddle and coach, the participants have been appreciative, analytical and critical; it can be quite a challenge sometimes, sea kayakers are an assertive bunch. I have endeavoured to include their good advice in this book. I am privileged to be associated with an international community of outstanding individuals who choose to travel the coastlines of the world in the smallest of boats.

This book describes the basic skills for efficiently paddling a sea kayak. All of the strokes described here are for paddling a typical modern-style paddle and a closed-deck sea kayak with a load of gear 25 kg or more. The underlying assumption is that the fundamentals of the basic paddle strokes are consistent across a wide variety of modern sea kayak designs and paddle shapes. Rudders, skegs and sails supplement but do not replace good paddling technique. In spite of this purposeful focus and arbitrary limitations I do not suggest that there is one best repertoire of paddling strokes, kayak design or paddle design. Selection of equipment depends a great deal on the kayaker's intent, whether to paddle in the marshlands or to traverse the outer coast.

Paddle strokes are described as a sequence of movements, body positions and manipulations of the paddle. While this is an acceptable and often preferred means to coach a beginner it is not the preferred end result for a capable paddler. The goal is for individual paddle strokes to blend into a smooth and effective personal paddling style. The pleasure of learning to paddle a sea kayak includes the opportunity to develop an efficient paddling style that enables you travel farther, faster, in comfort and safety.

This book does not cover the skills for any rescue or re-entry techniques nor does it cover the cognitive skills of trip planning, navigation or good judgment.

SEA KAYAK PADDLING

One of the joys of paddling a sea kayak is that within the first few minutes of sitting in the cockpit everyone can have fun and success. The techniques described in this book build on this obvious simplicity and describe a set of efficient paddle strokes that provide for a maximum of propulsion and manoeuvrability while using the least of the paddler's limited energy. When coupled with efficient paddling strokes, there is an optimal level of energy output that yields comfortable and quite remarkable progress. The capable paddler can travel a great distance and keep sufficient energy in reserve to deal with an unexpected delay or last minute difficulty before returning safely to the beach. The goal here is to develop paddling skills that allow each paddler to travel farther, faster, safer, while expending the least amount of energy.

↑ One of the joys of paddling a sea kayak is that within the first few minutes of sitting in the cockpit everyone can have fun and success.

Paddling a sea kayak is an activity of repeated paddle strokes. Good technique enables good progress and maintains good health. Poor technique can impede progress, strain joints, fatigue muscles and inflame connective tissues. Subtle corrections in the technique of repeated paddle strokes make an obvious improvement in the paddler's efficiency and durability. Two paddlers can reach the same destination at the same time; the one cruising comfortably arrives fresh and ready to continue, while the other one arrives exhausted and sore, in need of rest and an ice pack.

There are too many stories of individuals with copious amounts of energy that have paddled themselves and their companions into trouble. To make progress through unexpected difficult sea conditions sufficient energy must be accompanied by sufficient skill. Skill with the paddle represents just a fraction of the seamanship required to be a competent sea kayaker, but as I have already mentioned, this book is limited to the act of paddling.

Practical experience on the water is the best way to learn to paddle. The advice in this book is best applied in conjunction with good coaching and supportive paddling partners. There are businesses and associations that provide instructional programs to speed up the process of learning to paddle a sea kayak. During and after a course of instruction this book will serve as a guide to your practice.

INTRODUCTION

INTRODUCTION

Within the first few minutes of getting into a sea kayak and picking up the paddle, almost anyone can successfully paddle along the shore. Moving a sea kayak forward at three knots is easy, and this is part of kayaking's appeal. In 20 minutes a paddler can easily travel a mile down the beach or a mile offshore, being drawn ever onward by the scenery and wild-life. But there are many tales of inexperienced paddlers suddenly finding themselves in uncomfortable and dangerous situations, confronting unan-ticipated wind, waves or current. In good hands, the kayak is a remarkably seaworthy craft, capable of steady progress in even adverse sea conditions. But when the human propulsion system is inefficient or begins to break down, both paddler and kayak are in peril. In good hands, the kayak is a remarkably seaworthy craft capable of steady progress in quite awful sea conditions, returning home safely to venture out again on better days.

The techniques described in this book build on this obvious simplicity and describe a set of efficient paddle strokes. An efficient stroke provides a maximum of propulsion and manoeuvrability while using the least of the paddler's limited energy. The capable paddler can travel a significant distance and keep sufficient energy in reserve to deal with an unexpected delay or difficulty and then return safely to the beach. The goal of this book is to aid the paddler in developing the paddling strokes to travel farther, faster and safer, while expending the least amount of energy. Ideally this book accompanies a course of instruction led by a qualified coach.

Safety

→ Paddle with a partner.

→ Wear a personal floatation device well-suited for paddle sports.

→ Wear appropriate clothing for unexpected immersion.

→ Paddle in environments suited to your abilities; be cautious about the sea state and weather conditions.

Application

→ Have fun.

→ Challenge yourself.

→ Look beyond your kayak to the environment and all its inhabitants.

Key Points

→ The choice to travel by kayak is a choice to do more with less and to leave a gentle footprint where you tread.

→ Paddling is an activity that spans time, culture and geography.

→ Individually named strokes are meant to blend one into the other seamlessly, creatively and effectively.

Exercises

→ Paddle with friends, often.

→ Try new techniques, frequently.

→ Improve, continuously.

Repeated paddle strokes are the foundation for travelling in a sea kayak. Good technique encourages good progress and maintains good health, avoiding repetitive strain injuries. Consider the forward stroke, at a normal cadence of 25–30 strokes per minute (count one side). A three mile passage involves at least 1,500 paddle strokes. A small improvement in technique yields a large improvement in progress. Conversely, a small defect in technique repeated 1,500 times could make for tired muscles or sore joints. Poor technique can impede progress and lead to strained joints, fatigued muscles and inflamed connective tissues. Subtle improvements in paddle strokes increase the paddler's efficiency and endurance.

Practical experience on the water is the best way to learn to paddle. There is no one best repertoire of paddling strokes and no best kayak or paddle design. A great deal depends on the kayaker's intent—to paddle the marshlands or to traverse the outer coast or to adopt an indigenous regional paddling style. I invite all paddlers to begin with the foundations presented in these few pages and adapt them into their personal style and for their own purpose.

ENERGY, SKILLS AND JUDGMENT

The sea kayak is a human-powered craft and is not seaworthy if the paddler lacks endurance, skill or judgment. Given the organic union between paddler and kayak it is difficult to simply dissect the knowledge and judgment aspects of seamanship from the physical skills of handing the kayak, but that is essentially what this book proposes to do. This book is meant to be part of a larger library of resources. Moreover, text, video and other literary materials are by themselves insufficient and cannot stand on their own without paddling partners, coaches and abundant experience.

The paddler's body is the kayak's engine and it requires fuel and regular maintenance. Our safety depends on our human performance. Our fuels are food and water and all paddlers are susceptible to fatigue and dehydration. Efficient strokes use the least energy and keep up our energy reserves. Drinking and snacking while paddling will supplement our energy reserves but only a full meal and a good sleep will completely re-energize the paddler. Efficient paddling techniques reduce our energy consumption and increase the distance travelled. Over a period of several weeks of regular exercise the body will adapt to the demands imposed on it. As our skills improve with practice, the body's energy systems also learn to deliver energy in a more effective way. The result of skill and fitness is that we accomplish the same amount of work with greater ease and less energy. We can keep sufficient energy in reserve by starting with a full tank and conserving energy along the way.

Often the best way to deal with a hazard is to paddle around it or pass it by. Efficient paddling strokes are sustainable and require no great exertion. Making good speed upwind with each of those 1,500 strokes made in the last hour produced a maximum of propulsion with a minimum of effort.

Similar to maintaining adequate levels of energy reserves, paddlers must maintain adequate levels of skill in reserve. When sea conditions demand all the skill that is available then there is a real and imminent risk of serious harm. To hold a level of skill in reserve requires a balance between a no-nonsense understanding of one's own skill level, and a knowledgeable assessment of the sea conditions. Sea kayakers require

↓ Travelling by kayak is a physical activity that requires ample energy, skill and good judgment.

↑ Start your first sea kayak excursions by travelling with experienced friends during the more stable weather of the summer and keeping your journey within a large bay or inlet. Consider taking a course that involves overnight camping.

↓ Journeys out of the bay and around the protection of the headland require a significant investment in training and skill development. Good seamanship is based on considerable knowledge and judgment.

efficient and skillful paddling technique and must be able to modify their technique to suit changing conditions. A skilled paddler can progress through quite awful sea conditions. Preceding too many rescues are levels of paddling technique that do not meet the demands of the sea conditions.

Practice trains your body and thinking guides your practice. Skill and efficiency are the products of thoughtful practice and include the occasional excursion out to the edge of your comfort zone. A relaxed body can respond to the waves and the currents and a relaxed mind can make the decisions necessary for a safe passage. Learning to paddle a sea kayak safely and efficiently takes time, persistence and a little help. Paddle with people of greater skill than yourself and practice in safe yet demanding conditions. Physical skills develop slowly and improvement requires deliberate practice in a variety of sea conditions.

EQUIPMENT

Efficient paddling strokes involve the mechanics of a paddle and the capabilities of a human body. The human body is part of the equipment necessary to propel a sea kayak and it comes in as many shapes and sizes as kayaks and paddles. Having a personal paddling style is part of the joy of paddling. Like paddlers' faces, paddling styles are all the same and yet unique. The advice provided in this book describes the elements that are most common and can be applied most generally. Overlay personal preferences for equipment and paddling style onto a solid foundation that focuses on efficient technique.

PADDLES

Quick and efficient forward strokes and manoeuvring strokes are easier to perform with the paddle fully submerged in the water close to the kayak. A shorter paddle enables a higher cadence and encourages planting the paddle close to the kayak. Your height, the breadth of your kayak and your personal style of paddling will determine your preferred paddle length. For the best performance, choose a paddle length at the shorter end of your range of preference; I would suggest between 210–220 cm. A smaller paddle blade and a shorter paddle shaft may permit a higher stroke rate and provide better acceleration. If you have a paddle with a variable length you can experiment to find the best length that provides for a good cadence and ample power. I have found that paddles feathered between 30 and 45 degrees are ergonomically neutral requiring very little wrist twisting to counteract excessive feathering. Financial caution: As your paddling skill improves and your personal paddling style evolves be prepared for the rather strong tendency to buy new paddles and new kayaks. Be ready for the question, "Why do you have 3 different paddles?" The experienced paddler answers, "Because I just sold one."

↑ Good fundamental technique applies to a wide variety of paddle styles. David likes to paddle with a traditional Greenland-style paddle.

KAYAK

Some sea kayaks are 50 cm wide and 6 m long with a level keel line. These kayaks will track straight, keeping to a consistent heading, but are difficult to turn when off course. A kayak 60 cm wide, 5 m long with a rockered keel line will turn easily but require more control strokes to keep a straight course. Individual choice for a kayak design involves concerns for cost, durability, performance, fit and aesthetics.

FITTING IN THE COCKPIT

The cockpit of your kayak should allow you to paddle in comfort for an hour or more. Muscle power moves the paddle and the energy of the paddle stroke is transmitted back through the body to move the kayak. The seating arrangement should allow for comfort and the efficient transfer of energy. The cockpit of a sea kayak should fit the paddler's body loosely and comfortably but offer support when the paddler leans with the hips or lifts with a knee. Cockpits can be custom fitted with closed-cell foam pads to accommodate individual body shapes.

The energy generated by paddle stokes is transmitted back through the arms, shoulders and torso, to the buttocks, legs and feet. Efficient turning directs the paddle power laterally to the hull by means of the hips, knees and feet. Turning is most efficient when the paddler tilts the kayak on edge. Purposeful tilting also increases stability when paddling in waves or current. Controlled tilting requires contact between the hips at the sides of the cockpit seat, the top of the thighs at the cockpit rim, and the knees under the deck. Comfort and efficiency improve when there is support for the paddler's buttocks, hips, knees and feet.

A cockpit that fits the paddler encourages good posture and good posture is the foundation for all paddle strokes. With the feet placed on the footrests, adjust the footrest so that the legs are bent and the knees come close to or gently contact the deck. The seat and seat back should provide firm support for the lower back without restricting any motion. Proper support for feet, thighs and lower back are essential for sustained paddling.

When your body fits the cockpit you will stay in place when the waves are trying to shake you out of your seat. If a knee or hip slips out of place, or a foot comes off a footrest during a recovery-brace, the loss of secure contact with the kayak is almost certain to lead to a lot of water up your nose.

RUDDERS AND SKEGS

When deployed, a rudder or skeg changes the underwater profile of the kayak and its performance characteristics. When lowered, a skeg decreases the downwind drift of the stern and decreases weathercocking. It also increases tracking (travelling in a straight line) impeding efforts to turn the kayak. Lowered and held in a neutral mid-ship position a rudder decreases weathercocking in the same way as a skeg. Changing the angle of the rudder with the foot pedals provides steering control as long as the kayak has good forward speed. I have encountered numerous beginner paddlers stuck trying to paddle away from a lee shore with their rudder down, and little or no forward speed. In this situation their kayaks have excessive lee cocking making them quite unable to turn upwind and get away from shore. They could effect the desired turn by raising the rudder and allowing the stern to be pushed downwind. Rudders and skegs are excellent devices that supplement good paddling skills but their effectiveness relies on an understanding of how a kayak manoeuvres in the wind and waves.

In a moderate to rough sea state it can be difficult to maintain a steady downwind course. Wave crests arriving from behind accelerate the stern while the relatively still water of the trough slows the bow and the kayak persistently tends to twist (yaw) off course. Lowering a skeg has the advantage of decreasing weathercocking and increasing straight-line tracking. Course corrections are fewer and smaller. Using a rudder also reduces the number of course corrections and steering is very easy.

On a steady upwind heading having a rudder down decreases weathercocking but steering to counteract that effect might be a disadvantage. Similarly, it is usually most effective to retract a skeg while making an upwind heading.

Skegs are used to improve a kayak's tracking and counteract the forces of wind and waves as they work to push a kayak off course. Most sea kayaks will track well with the wind ranging from dead ahead 12-o'clock, to the side 2-o'clock or 10-o'clock. When making a course across or downwind the kayak may tend to weathercock or slew around in following seas. With the skeg lowered, the kayak will point downwind with less of a tendency to wander off course.

Rudders are installed to improve tracking and counteract the forces of wind and waves and to aide in turning. A rudder provides a wider range of control than a skeg and provides for additional manoeuvering.

Rudders and skegs do an excellent job of counteracting the forces that push a kayak off course but as mechanical systems, they occasionally fail, and it is my experience that they are most prone to break down when conditions are rough and the paddler is working the controls with some force. It is precisely at this time that manoeuvering control is critical. Learning to manage the kayak by tilting, without a reliance on a rudder or skeg, is useful for all paddlers. Tilting for steering works for sharper turns and manoeuvring in larger waves where sharper turns and greater overall performance are often necessary.

WHOLE BODY WORKOUT

Kayak strokes use the whole body, brains, brawn and timing. The coordination of our human resources is key to efficient strokes. Judgment and trained responses provide the best strokes at the right time. The hands, arms and shoulders function as part of the paddle and provide the initial power, timing and directional control. The torso provides the sustained power for strokes and braces. The hips, thighs, knees and feet are in contact with the boat to maintain balance and to transfer power to the kayak.

Consider swinging a baseball bat or golf club. The work of the swing must be coordinated amongst various body parts. The swing starts with a good stance and power is generated from the legs and rotation of the torso. The arms add power but serve largely to steer the swing and provide the

↑ Paddling home against the wind is a whole body workout that requires a good level of fitness.

more refined level of control. A kayak stroke is the same. Pick up a baseball bat, stand with your feet together, have your body face the pitcher, and swing the bat using only your arms, and keep your eye on the tip of the bat. It doesn't work very well. An effective paddle stroke, like an effective bat swing, starts from the legs, generates power through the torso, and is guided by the arms as you look where you are going. In the case of the paddle stroke and the swing of the bat, there is some initial practice of individual tasks of balance, power and steering, but in the end, a good stroke blends all the component parts into a single seamless, coordinated action.

WARM UP BEFORE EXERCISE

A warm-up is key to injury prevention avoiding the physical discomfort of sore muscles, and will lead to better overall paddling performance. Prior to any significant physical activity we should prepare the body for the forthcoming strains and stresses. A simple warm-up will accomplish many positive things. It will increase your heart rate, opening up small blood vessels and delivering more oxygen to your muscles. Warming up muscle fibers will increase the metabolism that converts the glycogen in your muscles into the energy that fuels them. Warmer muscles are also suppler, ready for the stretching and flexing of the paddling day. A warm-up that includes moving joints gently through a full range of motion will increase the production of synovial fluid that lubricates the bones and tissues within the joint.

The activities of a warm-up should actually warm up the muscles thermally, moving all joints and focusing a little extra on the muscles used most heavily in paddling: shoulders, torso, arms, neck and hips. Your legs have the biggest muscles in your body and are the most effective at increasing your heart rate and warming up your blood flow; so it seems that we should use all our muscles during the warm-up.

↑ With the wind comes the waves. A relaxed body with flexible hips and lower back lets the kayak move gracefully over the waves.

Early in the day the strenuous activities of lifting the kayak onto the roof of the car or van is the time that is likely to cause serious strain. This would suggest that a warm-up should occur well before the time we get onto the water. It also suggests that we should be most careful and ask for the help of our paddling partners while we are loading the kayak and heavy gear in and out of the car. A good quick short walk is an excellent way to warm up your body. Swing your arms and gently rotate and shrug your shoulders. Pause along the way to bend and rotate your neck and swivel your wrists and bend your elbows. Stand and gently twist your torso. Sitting in a kayak can be hard on the lower back and some extra time spent with simple back exercises is very sensible. Avoid forceful stretching; remember that the goal is to warm up before strenuous activity.

Once the car is loaded it may be a long trip to the launch site and the first piece of business will be to off-load the kayak from the roof of the car. At the launch site some repetition of the warm-up is appropriate. Once again, get assistance from your paddling buddies to lift and carry the kayak. The coldest time during a paddling day can be the last moments of the lunch break on the beach; consider re-warming before paddling away.

The injuries and strains that occur during the paddling day can often be traced back to the lack of a proper warm-up. Sore wrists, shoulders and lower backs that present problems during the day might be avoided by a timely warm-up routine.

COACHING HIERARCHY (STRATEGIC LEARNING)

For each stroke there are considerations for stance, rotation, choreography, tilt and application, and generally there is a strategic hierarchy that suggests we learn one aspect of a stroke before another. For example, to have good body rotation the paddler must sit up straight; stance comes before rotation.

Stance: Position of the body particularly as a starting position for each stroke.

Rotation: The rotation of the torso along the vertical axis of the spine.

Choreography: The compilation of movements which make up a stroke; the sequence of steps.

Tilt: The purposeful tilting of the hips and lower body that causes the kayak to tilt on edge along a horizontal axis.

Application: The correct circumstances for implementation.

Stance

To have good body rotation the paddler must have good posture and sit up in the kayak; posture comes first and rotation can then follow. In this context posture also refers to body position including arms and legs, head and torso.

The paddle shaft is gripped securely with relaxed hands spread at a width such that the forearms form a 90 degree angle with the shaft. This 90 degree angle should be approximated throughout most paddle strokes, and is referred to as the "paddler's box." The most power can be generated

↑ All strokes start with **good posture** that comes from strong core muscles. A seat and cockpit that fit your body provides the support necessary to be comfortable sitting up while you paddle.

when both forearms are approximately parallel. Orient your forearms so that one forearm is higher than the other. Consider how much power you can generate in a kayak stroke. While out paddling we will find ourselves ending up in all sorts of postures and positions but your next stroke of the paddle will be most effective if you start it by taking on the best stance.

↑ Jen has a good stance with forearms at right angles to the paddle shaft and approximately parallel to each other. Sitting up, her weight is centred over the kayak to keep her balance.

Legs

When paddling forward the power of the paddle is transmitted through the body to the footrests. Thighs and knees are supported under the deck and laterally by the side of the hull. When tilted, your legs, thighs and hips need to have enough support to control the kayak and avoid slipping out of place.

Rotation

Rotation refers to the orientation of the upper and lower torso. Upper torso rotation occurs when the body above the waist, and particularly the shoulder girdle, is rotated and the lower waist and hips remain still, such as when you turn your upper body when sitting in a dining room chair; the chair is still and the upper torso rotates. Lower body rotation occurs when the body below the waist is rotated and the upper body remains relatively still, as when your elbows are resting on a restaurant counter and you swivel the stool. The lower torso is encased in the kayak and turning the lower torso will turn the kayak; in some circumstances there is value in concentrating on moving the kayak with lower body muscles as opposed to moving the paddle with the upper body. On the slippery surface of the water it is not possible to completely isolate upper and lower torso rotation.

↓ The power of a forward stroke starts by reaching forward and rotating the upper body using the large muscle groups of the torso.

↑ Michael has planted his paddle in the water and rotated his upper torso into the direction he wants to turn. He will work to rotate his lower torso to turn the kayak against the resistance of the paddle blade.

↓ On the crest of a small wave, Andrew is turning to the right. With the paddle planted in the water he will work to rotate his lower torso to turn the kayak against the resistance of the paddle.

Choreography

Choreography includes the descriptive details of an isolated sequence of movements. For simplicity, each stroke can be described in isolation but this isolation rarely exists and the various named strokes must be linked and blended into the activity we know as paddling. Watching a skilled paddler we can see quite a remarkable ease of motion and efficiency of effort. Like an artful dance built of many steps, paddling is a skillful blending of many paddle strokes. Each step and stroke must be interpreted and is influenced by each paddler's strengths, weaknesses and preferences.

Gripping the paddle

Take the paddle in both hands and centre it. This grip is seldom changed and maintaining the same grip has the advantage of keeping you ready for any eventuality, but that is not an absolutely firm rule. There are techniques that work well with a different grip on the paddle.

↑ A proper grip on the paddle shaft is relaxed and secure and helps prevent the considerable discomfort of wrist tendonitis.

Each stroke begins with placing the paddle in the correct position relative to the paddler and the kayak. Attention must be paid to the fore and aft position of the paddle and the lateral position near or far from the side of the kayak. Not only must the paddle be in the correct position, it must have the correct angle of attack.

Placement

↑ All strokes start with the blade planted into the water at the right place. With her blade fully in the water, at a point near her feet, Jen is ready for the power phase of her forward stroke.

Angle of attack (paddle): The best angle of attack for the paddle blade is determined by several factors. In sculling the paddle moves through the water, but in the bow-rudder the paddle is held in position stationary against the flow of water. The flow of water can come as a result of the kayak moving through still water, or current moving past an idle kayak. Most frequently we encounter a combination of both. More simply, the angle of attack for a forward stroke is to have the blade facing aft, and for a sweep stroke that performs to turn the kayak, the angle of attack for the blade should face more outward than backward.

Timing and cadence

A stroke has two elements that involve the measurement of time. The timing of a stroke refers to the unfolding of a single stroke with attention paid to the sequential timing of actions. Cadence refers to the number of complete strokes per minute or, alternatively, how long it takes to link or blend a sequence of complementary strokes. The strokes may be a repetition of one kind of stroke as in many repeated forward strokes, or the linking of complementary strokes such as forward/sweep/bow-rudder/bow-draw/forward.

Tilt

Purposely tilting the kayak is part of efficient paddling. By lifting one hip and knee the paddler controls the tilt of the kayak, sometimes purposefully increasing the tilt to enhance performance and at other times working to oppose the tilting forces of waves or current.

Edging and leaning

← Manoeuvring and stability are greatly enhanced by purposefully tilting the kayak. James is demonstrating holding his kayak in a tilted balanced position on edge. Unseen inside the kayak he has tilted his hips and is lifting under the deck with one knee. Good seating and support for feet, knees, thighs and hips helps James keep control of his kayak.

↑ By leaning his head and body over the side of the kayak Nic has tilted beyond the point of balance. A lean-tilt is used for turning and bracing in current and waves and in those kinds of situations leaning actually increases your stability.

↓ The forward sweep stroke turns the kayak while contributing to forward momentum. Ian increases the effectiveness of the stroke by edge-tilting to the outside of the turn.

→ **Edge-tilt.**
Sitting upright and tilting the hips while raising one knee will put the kayak on its edge. Balance is maintained as long as the paddler's weight is over the buoyancy of the kayak.

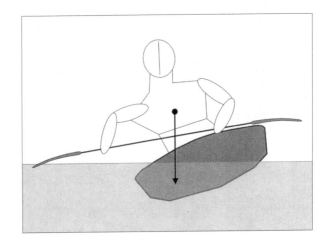

→ **Edge-lean.**
Leaning requires some external force to keep the kayak upright and stable. If the kayak is moving forward, as in a brace turn, lift is created as the paddle moves through the water.

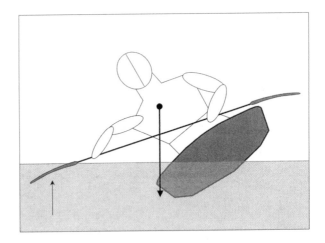

The lateral tilt of the kayak created by tilting the pelvis and lifting a knee is commonly referred to as "edging." When the left edge is lowered the kayak is "edged left." When a kayak is edged, the paddler's upper torso remains upright with the weight centred and balanced and the kayak is in a stable position. Leaning refers to tilting the kayak by means of the paddler leaning their upper torso over the side of the kayak; this creates an unstable tilted position. When the paddler is leaning, stability can be re-gained (or sometimes sustained) by means of bracing, sculling or judicious use of the force of moving water or waves.

24

EDGE CONTROL

EDGE CONTROL

↑ While paddling in moving water, Michael relies on good edge control for manoeuvring, balance and stability.

An understanding of controlled tilting (edge control) is fundamental to maintaining stability, turning efficiently and bracing. For all new paddlers there is a sense that stability comes from sitting upright and keeping the kayak on a level keel, but, like riding a bicycle, stability and turning requires some controlled tilting. While balance does include sitting upright, tilting the kayak improves the manoeuvrability of the kayak and adds stability when paddling in steep waves or fast current. Edging is a component of just about everything you'll want to do in a kayak. The absence of good edge control makes the paddler reliant on using the paddle for stability and balance. Stability in a kayak has more to do with controlling boat-tilt and body-lean than with support from the paddle. The boat should support your weight and the paddle is best used for propulsion and turning. (See photo on page 27.) Good edge control leads to greater performance and a great deal of fun. Turning a loaded sea kayak in wind and waves is a demanding task and any performance advantage is worth pursuing.

Edging and Leaning

Edging refers to tilting the kayak. Edging away from a turn is done to improve manoeuvrability, edging into a wave or downstream of a current is used to maintain stability, and edging into the wind helps keep the kayak on the right course. Edging is accomplished by lifting one knee and simultaneously lowering the opposite buttock; you can tilt the kayak and still keep your torso fairly upright with your head over the boat. This edges (tilts) the kayak and keeps your centre of gravity over the kayak. In circumstances involving large, steep waves and fast-moving current that threaten your stability, the kayak may need a more dramatic tilt to counterbalance the upsetting forces of the waves or current. The kayak can be given a dramatic edge-lean by moving your torso and head out away from the kayak's centre of gravity and using a brace stroke to maintain balance. (See Turning in waves, page 149.) When paddling a course across the wind the kayak may tend to make an undesirable turn upwind. Edging the kayak into the wind will help keep you on the desired course.

There are two skills involved in learning edge control. The first is finding the line that marks the transition between a balanced edge-tilt and an unbalanced edge-lean. The second part is choosing when to use a balanced edge-tilt and when to use an unbalanced edge-lean. Edging

← A good general rule is to rotate your body and face the direction that you intend to go. Ian is pulling his kayak sideways with a draw stroke and increasing the reach of his paddle by edging in toward his sweep stroke.

↓ To turn her kayak to the right Nancy edge-tilts and performs a sweep stroke on the left-hand side of the kayak. Edging to the outside of the turn will cause the kayak to turn efficiently to the right.

correctly is of great benefit but in rough sea conditions, a wet head often follows edging in the wrong direction.

For the moderate amounts of edge-tilt usually used to improve turning, sit upright, lift one knee (upper) and relax the other (lower) leg, keeping your weight centred over the kayak. A moderate degree of edging will usually put the hull-deck seam in the water. To edge left is to lower the left edge by raising the right hip and knee. While balanced with the kayak on edge, you will often want to continue paddling on both sides while manoeuvring the kayak with strokes over the raised edge. This is an unfamiliar posture and takes some practice before it feels like the right thing to do.

Safety

→ Keep your forearms near to right angles with the paddle shaft and keep the elbows near to your body and well bent. This posture keeps the shoulder joints in a strong and safe position, ready for a quick brace.

→ A relaxed grip on the paddle minimizes the stress on wrists and avoids the painful symptoms of wrist tendonitis.

Application

→ The most common turning stroke is the sweep and the effectiveness of the stroke is greatly increased by edging on the outside of the turn.

→ When heading in a generally upwind direction your kayak may tend to turn upwind (weathercock). Edging into the wind while paddling forward may offset the weathercocking effect of the wind.

→ When steep waves approach from the side, edging into the wave provides stability.

Key points

→ When edging, maintain your stability and balance by keeping your weight over the kayak and off of the paddle.

→ Edging requires you to keep an upright posture. Keep your back straight, sit upright and relaxed so that you can rotate your torso.

Exercises

→ Practice is key to developing good edging techniques and improvements in edging will greatly increase the overall effectiveness of your skills. There are no white lines down the centre of the watery road; take the opportunity to travel a less-than-straight course. Use mooring buoys, flotsam or any object on the water as an excuse to paddle a turning and twisting course. Practice making paddle strokes on both sides of the kayak while balanced and tilted. This is not intuitive or comfortable; keep practicing until it becomes second nature.

Sculling

Sculling is a motion of the paddle used to supplement many stokes such as the sculling draw, sculling low-brace, sculling high-brace and sculling for support. Sculling can be done with the front or back face of the paddle,

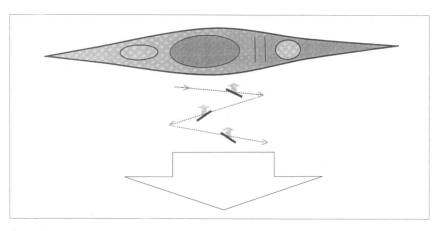

↑ Bird's eye view of the motion of the paddle blade for a sculling draw stroke. The paddle is stroked alternately towards the bow and stern. With each change of direction the angle of the blade is altered so that the leading edge of the blade is rotated away from the kayak causing the blade to pull on the water and draw the kayak toward the paddle.

with the paddle in a vertical or horizontal orientation. Sculling can even be done with the paddler in an upright or capsized orientation.

Sculling is a series of alternating strokes with the leading edge of the paddle at a slightly open angle of attack to gain a steady lifting force from the paddle. The motion of the paddle is much like that of a spatula spreading icing on a cake. Sculled horizontally near the surface (the top of the cake) the paddle provides support for balance and bracing. In a deep, more vertical position (the side of the cake), sculling is used to draw the kayak sideways. As the stroke alternates back and forth the leading edge of the blade changes and must be alternately raised to account for the change of direction. If the leading edge is raised too high the angle of attack is too steep and the paddle creates excessive turbulence.

→ The same back and forth sculling stroke that provides support can be used to manoeuvre the kayak sideways. Sculling with the paddle in a vertical position beside the kayak will draw the kayak sideways.

↑ Glynis demonstrates a sculling low-brace. Skimming the back side of the paddle back and forth across the water creates lift and support.

↓ In a sheltered cove, Nic is practicing his sculling. **Sculling** can halt a capsize and give Nic a moment to pause before he performs a high-brace and regains his upright position.

↑ James is practicing a technique called the **balance-brace**. He can rest in a stable position while lying motionless in the water, demonstrating that there is a great deal that one can learn about edge control.

BRACING

❷

BRACING

Bracing strokes are used for support and maintaining stability, or to recover from a capsize and regain stability. Bracing strokes are quite different from the strokes that manoeuvre the kayak. Good bracing skills can prevent a full-immersion capsize and the difficulties that follow. After a partial capsize, bracing returns the kayak to an upright position. A recovery from a capsize that wets only one ear can be called a brace. If both ears get wet, we can call it a roll. A successful brace is an understated self-rescue.

One good brace can prevent the need for a difficult rescue. In rough seas subtle braces blended into a forward stroke will give you the support that you may need to keep your kayak balanced and upright. In combination with edge-tilting towards a steep wave or downstream in a current, a well placed brace will keep the kayak balanced. Like bow-draw and stern-draw variations on the draw stroke, low-brace turns and high-brace turns are variations on the basic bracing strokes. When you lose your stability, bracing strokes are effective in limiting a capsize and can return you to an upright position from any position. Situations that unbalance the kayak often occur suddenly and braces used for support must be reflexive.

A brace stroke is a dynamic action that involves the entire body, the kayak and the paddle. From head to foot, the actions of the paddler's body make the brace work. The kayak must fit the paddler so that the kayak responds with the paddler's actions. The paddle can provide sufficient lift

↑ In most situations a low-brace is the first choice to keep the kayak stable.

↓ Practicing in calm water Nic has leaned over to the point of capsize and is performing a high-brace to recover.

↑ Roscoe is placing his paddle forward into the oncoming wave. His **high-brace**, placed toward the front of the kayak, will keep him stable moving forward against the oncoming wave.

↓ In the unsettling turbulent water Michael is ready to support his balance with a high-brace.

↑ Roscoe looks comfortable with a high-brace in the wave. While his kayak slides sideways he must keep leaning into the wave until the crest subsides in shallow water.

and support only when the body and the boat are working together. With the correct posture and a kayak cockpit that fits the paddler, there is very little lift or support required from the paddle.

Untrained paddlers react to the kayak becoming unstable by moving their heads away from the water, intuitively trying to avoid a capsize. This motion puts a curve in the back and causes the paddler's upper knee to push upward on the deck, increasing the tilt of the kayak and contributing to the forthcoming capsize. (See Hip-flick capsize on page 43.) As the kayak reaches the point of capsize, the beginner has a sense of being "locked" in place, unable to change their posture; capsize is inevitable. The natural reflex is to sit upright, raising the paddler's centre of gravity, adding to the kayak's instability; a full head-soaking capsize is underway. (See photo on page 46.)

Using bracing strokes to recover from a capsize is more about the hip-flick than it is about the paddle. In response to a capsize in progress, experienced paddlers will first tilt their heads toward the water and then, with the support of a bracing stroke, will hip-flick, sometimes very subtly, and recover their balance. Braces are effective at any point from having the edge of the spray deck in the water to having an ear in the water. To recover from a capsize the paddler will relax the head, neck and hips, then move the head towards the water and rapidly change the lifting pressure from the upper knee to the lower knee. (See Hip-flick recovery on page 44.) This quick motion of the hips and knees is hidden beneath the deck, and the uninformed observer notices only the flicking of the head and slapping the paddle. Relaxing the head to a position towards the water allows the important change of pressure from the upper knee lifting under the deck to the lower knee and this alone can be enough to return the kayak to a balanced position. To beginners it seems entirely illogical to prevent a capsize by moving their heads towards the water. However, without a change of head-tilt and knee-lift, recovery is nearly impossible and there is less support needed from the paddle than might be expected. (See photo page 46.)

Learning to brace is a circular problem; you need good bracing to be confident in rough water, and you need to be confident in rough water to develop good bracing. Practice begins with simulated capsizes in calm water and continues on to bracing in small waves. Skill with bracing develops with the experience of paddling in a variety of demanding sea conditions. Start this learning process in a pool or sheltered cove and then progress out into the wind and the waves. Good judgment is required in choosing conditions that are safe yet demanding enough to provide a useful learning environment. Good judgment is also required in choosing paddling partners that can help you learn and keep you safe as you explore the limits of your comfort and ability. Those paddling partners need to have the skill to rescue you when your practice exceeds your skill and things go wrong. This is where a good coach can select a demanding but safe location to try new skills or test existing skills.

BRACING IS NOT JUST ABOUT THE PADDLE

Stand on one foot and rise up onto the ball of your foot, as high onto your toes as you can stand. Swing your other leg forward, back and out to the side. Try twisting your hips quickly back and forth (still on one foot). Now, jump up as high as you can, returning onto the same one foot. You are doing very well if through all of this you do not have to put the other foot down to avoid losing your balance and falling to the floor. For practice, try it all one more time, then take a rest.

Now you can repeat the exercise but this time have a friend stand nearby with their arm extending out toward you with their hand reaching out palm up. Once again, stand on the ball of one foot and swing your leg. As you become a little unstable, use just one finger to brace onto the outstretched hand. With the one finger braced your balance improves remarkably and your ability to twist and jump is greatly enhanced. The counterforce provided by the single finger braced onto the helpful hand is small and, more importantly, it provides a great deal of mechanical biofeedback to enable you to keep your balance and move your body. This one little finger simulates the paddle brace.

If you were to grasp your friend's hand and the end of their out-stretched arm and lean on it heavily, without using your body muscles to maintain your balance they would be unable to hold you up and soon you would lose your balance and capsize to the ground; if you brace too heavily on your paddle it will submerge and you will follow. In the same way as the single finger provides improved balance and control, the appropriate gentle use of the paddle for bracing allows for considerable control of your body and the kayak. An over-reliance on the paddle produces unsatisfactory results.

Hip-flick

Hip-flick is the name commonly given to a motion not limited to the hips but involving most of the body. Like swinging a baseball bat (or golf club), good timing must come before power and an effective swing begins with stance, then execution and timing—and so does an effective hip-flick. Executed at the right time and in the right way, incorporating the muscles of the legs, hips, torso and shoulder girdle, a hip-flick can be subtle and very useful. In conjunction with an effective hip-flick a paddle-brace serves to provide some support and an important point of reference to orient the body. A hip-flick is most often associated with bracing and almost all braces must be accompanied by a well-timed and well-executed hip-flick. A swing of the bat or golf club develops its power from a good stance. Power develops from the legs and the torso rotating along with the swing

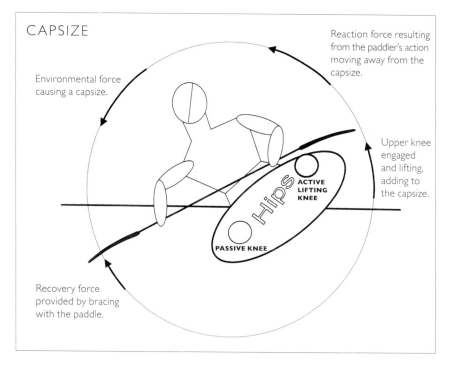

↑ **Hip-flick capsize.** The untrained paddler reacts causing increased instability.

When the kayak becomes unstable the untrained kayaker will tilt their head away from the direction of the capsize. The upper knee lifts on the deck, contributing to the capsize. There is also a natural reaction to sit upright, raising the centre of gravity and adding instability. The motion of the upper body away from the water works as a counter-weight and the kayak reacts by rotating towards the capsize. The kayaker has a sense of being "locked" in place, unable to move, and a capsize is inevitable.

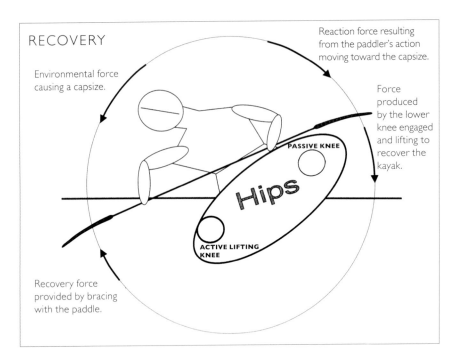

RECOVERY

Environmental force causing a capsize.

Reaction force resulting from the paddler's action moving toward the capsize.

Force produced by the lower knee engaged and lifting to recover the kayak.

PASSIVE KNEE

Hips

ACTIVE LIFTING KNEE

Recovery force provided by bracing with the paddle.

↑ **Hip-flick recovery.** The skilled paddler moves toward the water, the body is low and the kayak returns to a stable position beneath the paddler.

The head and upper body move to enable the movement of the lower body, lower the centre of gravity and provide a counterweight to the action of the lower body. Inside the kayak, the hips and knees move very little. When the paddler fits properly in the cockpit the kayak moves in response to the action of the lower body. The paddle-brace provides a point of reference for the body actions and some supportive force.

of the arms. Consider a swing with your feet together, torso facing forward, and only moving your arms—it would be awkward and entirely unsatisfactory. In the same way, all kayak strokes and hip-flicks are actions that require good timing and a cooperative division of labour amongst all of our major body parts.

To perform a hip-flick, relax your neck and move your head and shoulders toward the water. Relax the upper knee; raise the lower hip and lower knee. Practice in your living room by sitting on a desk chair or ottoman with your toes tucked under the sofa; gently and quickly lift one hip up and then relax. Your head and shoulders will most likely move slightly down and toward the hip that you are raising.

Moving the head a little forward toward the working knee will lower your centre of gravity and add to stability. It will also encourage the correct motion of the head and body toward the direction of the capsize, typically not an intuitive motion while sitting in a narrow kayak.

The head and upper body move to enable the movement of the lower body to set the kayak back on an even keel, as well as to lower the centre of gravity and provide a counterweight to the action of the lower body. The coinciding movements of head down, hip and knee up, is the "hip-flick." In response to a capsize, this almost simultaneous sequence of paddle-brace, relaxed-head, raise-the-hip-and-knee motion is counterintuitive and needs to be learned through training and practice.

The correct response to an imminent capsize is to tilt the head toward the water; the upper knee relaxes and the lower knee lifts, contributing to righting the kayak. Leaning forward, with the head moving toward the lower knee and closer to the kayak, will lower the centre of gravity, adding stability. The paddle-brace provides support and an important point of reference for the body actions of the hip-flick.

A successful brace relies on timing the hip-flick with the action of the paddle. The paddle performs two vital roles. It provides a counter-force to oppose the cause of instability, and gives a reference point for biofeedback so that the paddler's body can rotate the kayak back to a stable position. However, an overemphasis on using the paddle provides an unsatisfactory brace and can strain the shoulder, sometimes leading to a debilitating dislocation.

There is considerable momentum in a loaded sea kayak when pushed by a modest wave. When bracing into a breaking wave the paddler must balance a heavy load against the considerable force of the wave. A loaded sea kayak with paddler can easily weigh 250 pounds. To recover from a capsize and return to an upright position is almost effortless when done correctly. It is difficult and hazardous done incorrectly. Good technique is an important safety concern. Keep your elbows near to your body, rotate your torso if you need to brace to the back, and avoid reaching outward.

↑ Nic has capsized in calm water. His head is up and his (left) upper knee will be pushing up under the deck. Without a further response Nic will be upside down.

↓ Relaxing his head toward the water, Nic's (right) lower knee is engaged, lifting beneath the deck. With a hip-flick he will be upright, stable and on his way with his hair still dry.

→ Avoid vigorously flicking the head. The action is to move your hips to a position below your centre of gravity, not your head to a position over your hips.

Application

→ High-brace and low-brace capsize recovery.

→ Rolling.

Key points

→ Relax the head in a position tilted toward the water.

→ Engage the lower knee and relax the upper knee.

→ Relax your neck, lead with your shoulder and bring your head up last.

→ Use your hips more than the paddle; use the paddle but do not rely on the paddle for full support.

Exercises

→ Rehearse the correct form. Practice normal bracing stokes in calm water or very small waves. Working to perform your very best technique, you should be able to get near-perfect technique in non-threatening conditions. As your technique improves and you are able to hip-flick spontaneously the definition of calm water and small waves will change and you will be able to find comfort in increasingly choppy seas.

→ Use a small rigid paddle float to increase the range of your practice. The goal is to develop the very best technique; measure your success by how far you can tilt without losing control.

→ Measure your progress and success by how little you use the paddle. An effective hip-flick should be smooth and quick, without plunging the paddle.

Low-brace

A low-brace is done using the back face of the paddle blade. From a normal paddling position the hands are kept low and the forearms arms are in a near-vertical position; the grip on the paddle shaft does not change from a normal forward stroke. The paddler can reach the paddle out slightly with the offside hand no farther across the body than the belly button. Excessive reaching out or holding the paddle too near your waist will compromise the grip on the paddle shaft

A spontaneous low-brace is the quickest response to momentary upset. When the paddler is off-balance and needs to brace, the back of the paddle is placed flat on the surface on the side of the impending capsize. The paddle is held horizontal and low and can reach out on the side of the brace (set the offside hand near the belly button). The paddle is

↓ A low-brace is Glynis' response to an unexpected small wave near a shallow rock.

braced (pushed) onto the water, and aided by the support provided by the paddle, the paddler performs a hip-flick (see drawings on pages 43 and 44) to right the kayak.

A common error is to reach out too far. This is a sign that the paddler has a weak hip-flick and is relying too heavily on the support of the paddle. It also weakens the grip and exposes the offside shoulder to possible injury. The grip is further weakened if the paddle is held too close to the paddler's body. In this case the paddler's box has collapsed.

In reaction to a sudden off-balancing a quick low-brace usually results in the paddle making an audible slap on the surface. Sometimes called a slap-brace, the slapping action provides additional force to slow an imminent capsize and an extra moment for the paddler to hip-flick the kayak back to an upright position.

↓ Ian is safe and comfortable with a low-brace in a breaking wave. His low-brace is quite sufficient to keep him upright and is less stressful on his shoulders than an unnecessarily aggressive high-brace. With the paddle placed toward the stern of the kayak, the bow is free to be pushed by the wave and he might surf forward with the progress of the wave.

A low-brace can be used to maintain or regain stability when you encounter a steep wave. A surf wave or a wind-generated wave moves ahead at considerable speed and will either pass under the kayak or push the kayak along with the crest. Waves created by current flowing from shallow to deep water or over other irregular bottom features will force waves that occur in one place and are called standing waves. The standing wave remains in one place while the kayak moves with the current through the wave. The bracing response is the same; the paddler leans and braces into the crest of the wave.

↑ Braces are often blended into other strokes. Jen is heading into a current that creates some small standing waves. Her low-brace to the stern has elements of a stern-rudder stroke. She can keep her balance with the low-brace and turn the kayak with the stern-rudder.

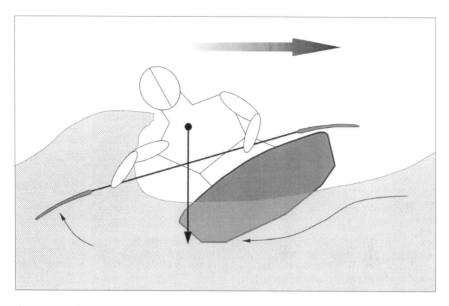

↑ Stable low-brace on wave. Leaning into a breaking wave, the motion of the kayak being pushed over the water helps stabilize the kayak. The same result occurs in current where the water is moving and the kayak may remain relatively stationary.

↓ Unstable low-brace on wave. Leaning away from a breaking wave, the motion of the kayak over the water works to forcibly capsize the kayak. The same result occurs in a standing wave where the water is moving and catches the edge of the kayak.

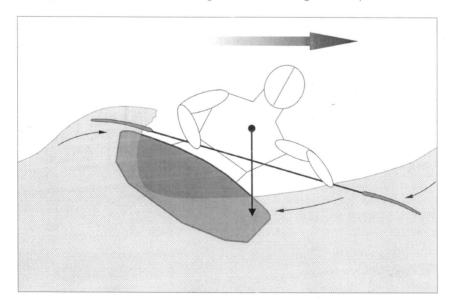

SCULLING LOW-BRACE

A sculling low-brace can provide continuous support. When rescuing a swimmer onto your back deck or while sitting in turbulent water steady support can be achieved with a sculling low-brace. The back face of the paddle is sculled back and forth over the surface to provide the motion for continuous support. (See Sculling, page 31.)

Safety

→ Keep the paddle approximately centred in front of your body.

→ Work to maintain the paddler's box as best you can. The paddle should be in front of and near parallel to a line drawn through the shoulders.

→ If the paddle needs to go toward the stern, rotate your body. Avoid extending your shoulder and arm to the back.

Application

→ The low-brace should be your primary response to most threats to stability.

→ Bracing is the first line of defence against turning a simple capsize into a complicated rescue.

Key points

→ Keep a good upright sitting posture with loose hips and a flexible spine.

→ Relax your neck and tilt your head toward the water.

→ Perform a hip-flick at just the right time; relax, paddle-brace and hip-flick in quick succession.

Exercise

→ At the edge of a sandy beach have a partner straddle the bow of your kayak. They will hold onto your perimeter lines or other handhold.

The partner can suddenly tilt your kayak and you should respond with a properly executed low-brace.

→ Rehearse the correct sequence of motions. Make small pretend capsizes and then perform a proper low-brace.

→ Use a small paddle float to add some security and a wider range of motions during your capsize rehearsals. A small float provides sufficient security, and if your brace is poor it will sink, showing you that you are using too much force and not enough technique.

↑ A small foam paddle float is an excellent practice aide for bracing, sculling and rolling. A small float provides only enough additional support for Glynis to practice good technique without relying on too much support from the float.

↑ Fully capsized, a sculling high-brace can be practiced easily with the aide of a small foam paddle float. A great deal of confidence is gained by practicing support and recovery techniques in the transition zone between upright and underwater.

↑ A homemade rigid foam paddle float, made from two pieces of one-inch-thick high-density "etha-foam" wrapped with electrician's tape.

THE FOAM PADDLE FLOAT AS A TRAINING AID

A small homemade rigid foam paddle float is a great aid when practicing bracing and rolling. The paddle float is made of two pieces of 2 cm-thick rigid white polyethylene foam approximately 20 cm x 40 cm wrapped in electrician's tape. Bevel the edges of the foam at the opening to make the paddle enter the float easily. Storing the float on a small stick will create a slightly open shape and aid in drying the float.

High-brace

A high-brace is done with the front face of the paddle and the hands are usually higher than the elbows. The grip on the paddle shaft does not change. To keep your shoulders in a strong and safe position you must keep your hands low (below your shoulders) and your elbows in near your body.

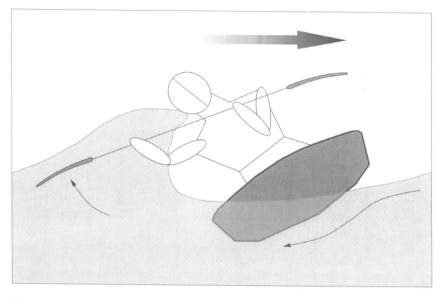

↑ Stable high-brace. Leaning and bracing into a wave approaching from the side. When using a high-brace it is important to keep the elbows low and close to the body.

The high-brace is used when the angle of capsize is substantial or when a wave is cresting above chest height. The front face of the paddle is placed out to the side of the capsize, the shaft held as horizontal to the surface as possible with the elbows low and tucked into the body to protect the shoulders from injury. The lower body rights the kayak under the paddler. Head position—generally cocked over the raised knee—is important for balance in the high-brace.

When used to recover from a capsize a high-brace can have a deep paddle with a more vertical angle. In this deep and vertical position, the

↑ As the wave arrives a high-brace and a little lean into the wave will let it pass uneventfully.

↓ Roscoe has rotated his upper torso and placed his high-brace toward the stern, and the bow is free to be pushed by the oncoming wave. It is likely that the kayak will turn to the left and Roscoe will surf forward with the wave.

paddle is pulled toward the kayak and the paddler performing a hip-flick in the usual way generates the bracing action of the paddle.

During a forward stroke the moment of "the catch" can be turned into a high-brace merely by rotating the paddle. The paddler rotates the wrists back and the stroke turns into a high-brace.

The expression "the more I practice the luckier I get" has a measure of truth in it. Having practiced and developed confidence in rough water, the capable paddler is prepared to place a pre-emptive supporting brace into a threatening wave rather than using a recovery brace after an upset.

SCULLING HIGH-BRACE FOR SUPPORT

A sculling high-brace for support will keep you upright if your kayak is at rest in calm water or it can give a moment of relative stability to regroup and regain control. When skilled paddlers find the need to scull it is often done only very briefly, with just one or two strokes of the paddle. The added momentary support from a sculling high-brace can give them time to regain their composure and continue on.

During a moment of static support while capsized and sculling, the paddler has the upper knee engaged under the deck and the lower knee is relaxed. To upright the kayak and recover stability the work of the knees is reversed in the performance of a hip-flick. The upper knee must be relaxed and the lower knee is engaged and actively lifts under the deck (hip-flick).

The beginner may have difficulty making the transition from sculling for support to a sculling high-brace for recovery. During sculling for support the upper knee engages the deck and the lower knee should be relaxed—the paddler is said to hang from the upper knee. If this knee slides out of place the paddler is sure to loose all support and capsize into the water. Static support while hanging from the upper knee is the exact opposite to the knee action for performing a sculling high-brace for recovery. Switching action and control from the upper supporting knee to the lower recovery knee is not always an easy thing

↑ Nic is practicing a sculling high-brace to halt a capsize. He will relax his head and neck, and hip-flick to recover the kayak to an upright position.

↓ Rather than the extra effort required to hold her head out of the water, Glynis has capsized onto the surface. For extra leverage and support she has extended the length of her paddle by altering her grip. Her right hand is near the paddle blade and her left hand is near the centre of the shaft. A little sculling, high-brace and hip-flick and she will recover from the capsize.

to do. The exercise of extreme sculling with your ear in the water is a way to practice this.

Rotate your upper torso away from the direction of capsize. Start sculling for support, lay back and swing your torso into the water with as much of the offside shoulder in the water as possible—you want the back of your head in the water. You will be holding yourself in your seat with the aid of your upper knee. To finish the exercise, perform a hip-flick and high-brace; you will have to make the transition from support with the upper knee to lifting with the lower knee. Extreme sculling with your ear in the water is sometimes dismissed as a trick stroke or just an exercise for practice; however, the stroke does provide the opportunity to use the lower body to control the boat in the tilted position and then bring it back to an upright and stable position. A capsize need not result in an inverted seated position with water going up your nose. You will be quite pleased if you can stop the capsize with a brace, pause to regain control by sculling and then brace again to an upright position. Remember it is more about control and timing of your body than it is about splashing about with the paddle.

Move the paddle back and forth in slow, wide arcs with minimal splashing. Practice the sculling motion as if you were spreading icing on a large cake. Avoid hanging from the paddle shaft as you scull. Use your hips, knees and feet in contact with the interior of the kayak, along with good upper body posture to balance the kayak in equilibrium. Minimize the forces causing the kayak to capsize by offsetting them with enough force from the stroke to keep everything in balance.

Safety

→ Keep the paddle in front of your chest. Your paddle blade should be easily within sight; rotate your shoulders and torso as needed. Many shoulder injuries can be attributed to poor technique when using an extreme high-brace and extreme sculling. During an anxiety-driven response to a sudden capsize the inexperienced paddler will extend the working arm and stroke the paddle too far toward the stern. In this posture the shoulder is very weak and prone to dislocation or other injury. Frantic efforts by the paddler to keep their head above water will lead to extra effort exerted when the shoulder is in this weak position. The paddler confident in leaning, bracing and rolling can relax, regain a safe posture and recover comfortably and efficiently.

Application

→ Recovering from a significant angle of capsize.

→ Maintaining stability when steep waves are working to tip the kayak.

→ A high-brace is the essential part of a kayak roll.

→ Sculling can provide the extra lift to finish a near-successful brace or the momentary support to brace instead of having to roll.

→ Bracing is the first line of defence against turning a simple capsize into a complicated rescue.

Key points

→ Try and maintain a right-angle between your forearms and the paddle shaft.

→ Keep the paddle in front of your chest.

→ Keep the paddle generally centred without too much reaching outboard of the kayak.

→ Relax your neck, lead with your shoulder and bring your head up last.

→ Use your hips more than the paddle; use the paddle but do not rely on the paddle for full support.

→ Have a cockpit and seat that provides good support for your hips, knees and feet.

Exercises

→ Rehearse the correct form. Practice sculling in calm water or very small waves. Working to perform your very best technique, you should be able to get it near perfect in non-threatening conditions.

→ Scull with the front side of the paddle and smoothly switch to using the back side of the paddle.

→ Use a small paddle float to add some security and a wider range of motion during your capsize rehearsals. A small float provides sufficient security, and if your brace is poor it will sink, showing you that you are using too much force and not enough technique.

→ Try to perform a balance brace with the support of a paddle float.

→ A brace does not require the paddle to be on the surface. Place the paddle slightly below the surface and pretend a minor capsize. Use the paddle in its submerged position for bracing support and hip-flick to recover. Try it again with the paddle a little deeper; eventually you can learn to brace with the paddle near vertical.

FORWARD STROKE

❸

FORWARD STROKE

Sea kayaking is principally a forward paddling activity and the forward stokes deserve attention to detail. Small improvements in the forward stroke are subtle and the effect may not be immediately apparent, but when repeated 3,000 times an hour (count both sides), the outcome becomes obvious. An efficient forward stroke propels the kayak at the best speed with the least effort and the most comfort. An efficient forward stroke provides good progress and takes into consideration our limited but renewable biomechanical energy. Slow progress exhausts the paddler by taking too much time, and efforts to travel too fast cannot be sustained. Attention paid to good technique avoids uncomfortable joint pain or debilitating inflammation in wrists, elbows or shoulders. A superficial glance would suggest that the arms are the principal engines driving the forward stroke. A sustainable forward stroke develops from the muscles of the legs, lower torso, upper torso, shoulder girdle and finally, the arms.

Hold the paddle with a relaxed grip, hands spaced slightly more than shoulder width apart, equal distance in from each end of the shaft. A relaxed grip reduces the possibility of repetitive strain injuries such as wrist tendonitis. Holding the paddle in this way forms a rectangular box—chest and upper arms, forearms and paddle shaft. Approximate right angles are formed at the elbows and between the forearms and paddle shaft. The paddler's box deforms during the execution of all strokes but in most cases

↑ Pushing and pulling, Ian is paddling forward with his "paddler's box" intact. As the right blade exits the water the left blade is almost set up for the next stroke. His paddling style has his hands in a moderate position not significantly high or low.

too much distortion is detrimental to the efficiency of the stroke and the physical safety of the paddler.

An upright sitting posture allows the torso rotation that can incorporate the large torso muscles into the stroke. The spine should be near vertical, possibly with a slight forward lean.

When sitting upright, the work of the stroke is efficiently transferred to the kayak through the feet. Ensure the feet are firmly placed on the footrests, allowing the efficient transfer of energy from the body to the kayak. A slouching posture not only inhibits torso rotation but it places the paddler in a relaxed posture and the transfer of paddle energy to the kayak is like trying to drive a nail with a rubber hammer.

↑ Karen is paddling with a forward stroke technique that has the hands low near the deck. She is using a carbon fibre bent-shaft narrow bladed paddle. It is a modern version of the simple wooden Inuit style paddle David uses on page 9 and James uses on page 34.

↓ Michael is moving quickly forward with a high-angle stroke typical of performance paddling. Efficient paddling includes the ability to adapt your paddling style to suit changes in weather and sea state.

The forward stroke has two sides, each with four significant parts: the set-up, the plant, the power and the exit. It is important to note that this breakdown into four parts is entirely artificial and one part of the stroke leads to the next in a continuous blend of motion of symmetric left and right forward strokes.

SET-UP FOR A RIGHT-SIDE FORWARD STROKE

The set-up is the portion of the stroke when both paddles are out of the water. For the set-up, we will focus our attention on the forward paddle that is about to enter the water. It is important to note that a last part of the stroke, the exit, comes immediately before the set-up. In this way a proper exit leads to a proper set-up; the two parts of the stroke are physically joined by the paddle shaft.

Reach forward by extending your right arm and moving the right shoulder forward. This will cause the upper torso to twist. Twisting the torso is similar to winding a spring and loading it with energy. The right arm should be almost straight with the torso slightly rotated. In general, for any stroke it is important to always keep the elbows bent, at least a little, even when reaching. Straight elbows are prone to chronic repetitive strain discomfort or traumatic hyperextension injury.

Reaching forward and twisting slightly sets up the paddle to be planted into the water as far forward as comfortably possible. Plant the paddle into the water somewhere near the feet (think of using the upper hand to plunge the entire blade forward into the water). Avoid using the lower hand to place the paddle in the water because this action tends to draw the paddle aft. Bend the lower elbow and begin the power phase when the paddle is completely immersed.

↑ The power of Karen's forward stroke starts as she reaches forward to place the paddle into the water. Reaching forward also rotates the upper torso and that incorporates the large torso muscles into the power of the stroke. The energy generated by the torso muscles can be sustained for a longer time than using the arms alone.

↓ Moving upwind, Jen demonstrates a more vertical style stroke than Karen.

↑ The blade is not planted fully into the water and not sufficiently far forward; very little power will be generated by this stroke.

EDGE

While paddling forward the kayak is normally sitting level in the water. However, in a cross wind, steep waves or current, the paddler will edge-tilt the kayak to maintain stability or offset the undesired turning effects of the wind and waves. (See Paddling in the wind, page 142.)

CATCH

The catch is the moment just after the paddle is planted in the water when the power phase begins. This moment will start winding your torso rotation and should place the right foot firmly against the footrest. With the paddle fully immersed it will catch firmly in the water and you can experience pulling the kayak forward. In calm water, both feet rest comfortably on the footrests, but when power is required, pushing with the power-side foot enhances power and torso rotation.

↑ Ian is taking a relaxed pace and showing good fundamentals. His upper forearm is approximately level providing him a good lever to push the paddle forward with arms and torso. The path of the paddle starts near the kayak and moves outward slightly. Here Ian's stroke is generally following the line formed from the bow wake.

POWER

Most of the power in the forward stroke is developed during the first third of the paddle's travel through the water, so a quick and complete plant and catch is essential. As the torso rotation continues, bend the right elbow and return to its neutral angle of about 90 degrees. The path of the paddle is slightly angled away from the side of the kayak. This angled path promotes torso rotation and keeps the paddle from diving unnecessarily deep. There is no need to think about pushing or pulling the paddle; this comes naturally. The power comes from torso rotation, with an emphasis on good posture and using torso muscles for the stroke. During the power phase

↑ Michael's aggressive sprint shows the same good fundamentals as Ian's relaxed pace (on page 71). For increased power he is leaning forward, and has his torso well rotated to increase his forward reach and power. A powerful stroke is generated by torso muscles working with the legs for maximum power. A high cadence will provide the power and speed to paddle through a wave or a strong current.

the left (upper) hand should travel a nearly horizontal path, independent of a high-angle or low-angle style of stroke. The power phase ends with the right paddle near your hip and the left near the centreline to the kayak.

EXIT

To lift the paddle from the water raise the wrist and elbow together. There is very little wrist or elbow flexion and the left forearm is in a good posture to push ahead for the forward stroke. The proper exit can be considered the beginning of the stroke because it sets up the new power hand ready for the next stroke.

It is easy to observe that during the power phase of the forward stroke

↑ Exiting the paddle from the water sets up the next stroke. The elbow and hand should rise at the same time with the forearm in a posture ready to push the paddle forward. It is evident that Ian is rotating his torso with each stroke to add power and endurance.

↓ Nic demonstrates a common example of poor technique. The paddle has been lifted from the water by rotating the arm (lifting the hand only). This leaves Nic in a weak position to push his paddle forward and the paddle will not enter the water in a position well forward.

↑ Flexing the wrist with each lift of the paddle can lead to unnecessary joint stress.

the offside hand travels in a nearly horizontal path. This is true for a low-angle or high-angle style of paddling. An offside (upper) hand travelling in a nearly horizontal path is in a good posture for the pushing part of the forward stroke and encourages the important and much talked about torso rotation. There is limited power available when the wrist rises substantially above the elbow and the paddler will naturally lower the working hand into a position more closely horizontal to the elbow. Unfortunately by the time this has happened the best part of the power phase is over.

CADENCE

To keep the kayak moving forward at good speed and efficient cadence is about 25–30 strokes (on one side per minute). Going slowly is never a problem but to maintain a speed of 3–4 knots the paddle must be in the water as often as possible. It works much better to paddle with equal force more often than to paddle at the same cadence with more force. The kayak slows down each moment that a paddle is not in the water and it is harder to regain the lost speed than keep up good speed in the first place. An efficient forward stroke is short, strong and quick. Like running up a hill, we should shorten our stride and quicken our pace. It takes some deliberate practice to get used to paddling with a quick cadence.

Safety

→ Maintain good upright sitting posture to avoid lower back strain. A seat and cockpit that fits your body providing foot braces, knee and thigh support are key to providing your lower body the points of contact necessary for good posture.

→ During the exit portion of the forward stroke lift the paddle with the aid of your upper arm and shoulder. Keep your forearm closer to horizontal than vertical. Repeatedly pushing your paddle forward with your hand high and your elbow low puts unnecessary strain on your shoulder.

→ Good exit technique helps limit excessive wrist flexion and the accompanying repetitive strain injuries (wrist tendonitis).

→ Feather your paddle to provide an ergonomic set-up that reduces wrist and elbow flexion and minimizes repetitive strain injuries. For most paddlers, a paddle can be feathered between 15 and 45 degrees.

Application

→ An efficient forward stroke moves the boat forward at the best speed with the minimum of effort and maximum of comfort.

Key points

→ Paddle out in front of your chest.

→ Plant the paddle quickly and fully.

↑ Glynis is exaggerating the torso rotation of a forward stroke by tapping her paddle right blade on the left edge prior to a right-side stroke and then following on the other side for the next stroke. After 20 exaggerated practice strokes she will continue on by paddling normally but will have a good feeling for incorporating some rotation into her normal stroke.

→ A high cadence and high-angle style of forward stroke is suitable for bursts of speed while a lower cadence and lower-angle style of power phase is suitable for cruising. You will need to use high-angle and low-angle styles to balance your needs for power, speed and endurance.

→ Pay attention to the exit phase of the forward stroke. It is very influential in leading to an effective set-up and plant, but often neglected.

Exercises

→ To get the feeling of torso rotation in the forward stroke, exaggerate the set-up, reach and plant portion of the stroke. To start with a right-side forward stroke reach well forward and across the deck to tap-tap your right-side paddle blade on the left deck seam of your kayak. Start with a rectangular paddler's box then reach forward with the elbow still partially bent. Perform a right-side plant and complete the stroke. The exit should be followed by a tap-tap of the left-side blade on the right-side deck seam. Repeat 20 times then paddle normally.

→ Check your normal cadence. For 5 minutes, count your right-hand strokes. Many experienced paddlers have a cadence of 25 or up to 30 in one minute.

• Reverse Stroke

Although you will use the reverse stroke for only very short distances it is still very useful. The fundamental concepts of the forward stroke can be freely applied to the reverse stroke. Paddling backward is usually done to manoeuvre in close quarters and it is important to turn around and look behind you. Good torso rotation helps with the power of the stroke and helps with the twisting necessary to occasionally look where you are going.

The paddle is planted aft and then stroked forward, passing through the water further away from the kayak than it does for the forward stroke. This wider placement adds a measure of support to the reverse stroke and compensates for the natural instability of moving backwards and twisting around to see where you are going.

Steering the kayak while moving backwards is less intuitive than paddling backward in a straight line and some practice will help alleviate the accompanying disorientation. In addition to the simple manoeuvring in close quarters, the reverse stroke comes into play when paddling in sea conditions that include current and breaking waves. Slowing down to avoid accelerating and surfing down a steep wave, and backing up in current to assist in turning are two situations where skillful application of a reverse stroke is very helpful.

↑ Nic rotates his upper torso to look where he is going and to put power into his reverse stroke. Paddling and looking backwards can be a little unstable and typically the paddler uses the back of the paddle to blend a bit of low-brace into the reverse stroke.

↓ A reverse stroke is an important part of manoeuvring the kayak. Michael is backing out of the main current and across a turbulent eddy line. As the stern enters the eddy the main current moving left to right will quickly swing his bow around and he will be facing downstream (to the right).

→ In reverse, navigate a passage between mooring buoys or other floats. Paddlers have to really twist around to see where they are going.

→ When rescuing someone who has capsized close behind you, it is quicker to paddle backwards rather than turning about to paddle forward. Back out of surge channels, caves or other confined spaces that are too narrow to turn around in. Alternately you can back into a tight space, keeping a watch for incoming waves, and be ready to move out quickly with a forward stroke. Backing onto a beach with a small breaking wave is good practice—touch the beach with the stern of the kayak and then paddle out again away from the beach; repeat.

Stopping

Stopping a kayak is a modification of reverse paddling. The paddle is planted at an aft position near the paddler's hips and to keep the kayak from turning a short modified reverse stroke is performed. From any speed you should be able to stop the kayak with three quick strokes on both sides. To add some stability, the end of the reverse sweep portion can approximate a low-brace.

SWEEP STROKES

4

SWEEP STROKES

Forward sweep

The forward sweep stroke is the fundamental stroke for turning a sea kayak. The sweep is a modified forward stroke and adds to forward momentum as well as causing the kayak to turn. A sweep stroke on one side should be followed by a forward stroke on the other side. Consider a turn to the right. The stroke is set up with an initial upper torso twist to the right and the left paddle planted well forward on the left side of the kayak. During the stroke, you unwind the lower torso to turn the kayak against the resistance of the paddle. At the end of the sweep, withdraw the paddle from the water quickly or it will act as a stern-rudder and reduce the momentum of your turn.

PLANT
Sit up and lean forward to plant the left paddle in the water as far forward as comfortably possible. The left arm is low and extended with the elbow slightly bent. The angle of attack on the paddle faces more outward than the forward stroke. This more open angle will direct the force of the stroke in a turning direction, pushing the bow of the kayak away from the front face of the paddle. Look where you are going with your chest in the direction you want to go.

↑ Heading upwind Michael has his blade planted well forward, the kayak is edged to the outside of the turn, his torso is rotated and he is looking where he is headed. Against the resistance of the paddle planted in the water he will work to unwind his lower torso into the direction of the turn. Pushing the paddle with his upper hand will also counter-rotate his upper torso.

EDGE

The kayak is edge-tilted to the outside of the turn; edge left, sweep left will turn you to the right. Edging the kayak in this manner will cause the kayak to turn on its own, decreasing the effort required to turn the kayak. Sea kayaks have a substantial length and can be hard to turn. The sweep stroke is the second most frequently used stroke, second only to the forward stroke.

CATCH

As in the forward stroke the catch is the moment just after the paddle is planted in the water when the power phase begins. This motion starts your torso rotation and should have the left foot firmly against the footrest.

↑ Turning to his right Ian is in the middle of a sweep stroke; he is committed to the direction of his turn. His left sweep and left edge-tilt will turn his kayak to the right.

When the paddle is fully immersed it will catch firmly in the water and you can experience pushing the bow to the right sideways through the water.

POWER

With the paddle caught firmly in the water think about pushing the kayak in the direction of the turn using your legs, unwinding your lower torso in the direction of the turn. After the catch, the path of the paddle should sweep an arc outward and your upper torso will counter-rotate against the turn. Your hands remain low to accentuate a widely arcing stroke. A longer, slower stroke with minimal splashing is more effective than a quick, short, splashing stroke. However, once the stroke is complete the paddle should exit the water quickly.

The sweep stroke uses only one blade, but we can use both blades to enhance the turn. For more turning power use both ends for the paddle and combine two different turning strokes into a smooth sequence. (See Combined strokes for turning, page 141.)

EXIT

At the end of a sweep stroke the paddle exits the water in the same manner as the forward stroke. Raise the wrist and elbow together with the forearm in a good posture for the next forward stroke. The paddle should be exited as soon as the stroke is complete. Delaying the exit leaves the paddle in a position as a stern-rudder and will work to turn the kayak in the wrong direction.

↑ Michael is at the end of a left sweep stroke, and to keep up his forward momentum he is about ready for a forward stroke on the right. To continue his turn he will keep his left edge-tilt and follow his forward stroke with a second sweep stroke.

EXTENDED PADDLE

When more leverage is desired you can change your hand position and take an extended grip. An extended grip is commonly used in a pivot turn starting from a stationary position.

↑ Altering her grip on the paddle Glynis has added leverage for an extended paddle sweep stroke. This is a useful technique when turning the kayak starting from a stationary position.

Reverse sweep

The reverse sweep significantly reduces forward momentum and is best used for stationary turning (pivot) or when you want to concurrently slow down and turn the kayak.

To start the reverse sweep stroke, plant the paddle in the water well to the stern of the kayak. The back face is the working side of the paddle. Rotate your upper torso strongly to the back and look where you want to go. Complete the stroke in the same general manner as the forward sweep.

Avoid using a stern-sweep in situations where you are working to keep the kayak moving forward. A common problem is to over use a reverse sweep to compensate for a weak forward sweep. Making course corrections with a reverse sweep is often the cause of poor forward speed.

↑ The reverse sweep is often used for turning starting from a stationary position. Nic's upper torso is fully rotated into the direction of the turn. Against the resistance of the paddle blade in the water he can unwind his lower torso into the turn.

↓ Nic is using a series of reverse sweep strokes to turn while moving backward. Every couple of strokes, while moving in reverse, turn and look where you are going.

Safety

→ Avoid excessive reaching and extension of the shoulder or elbow. When the arm is extended the elbow should be slightly bent.

→ For a sweep stroke the blade should be planted in a position well forward, and the forward arm reaches out into a nearly straight position. As the power portion of the stroke commences the elbow should return to a more bent position.

Application

→ The sweep stroke is the primary turning stroke used to turn the kayak and blends into the forward stroke to make ongoing course corrections.

→ For a right turn think edge left, sweep left turns right.

→ The sweep stroke turns the kayak while maintaining forward momentum.

→ Stationary pivot turns are performed with forward and reverse sweeps, commonly with an extended paddle grip.

Key points

→ At the set-up, look and rotate your upper torso in the direction of travel. Work to unwind your lower torso, pulling your body and kayak into the turn. Your upper torso will naturally counter-rotate against the direction of the turn.

→ Planting the paddle well forward is aided by a slight forward lean.

→ Make sure the paddle is planted with a slightly open angle of attack. At the beginning of the power phase of the stroke, sweep the paddle out and away from the kayak.

→ Edge the kayak away from the turn, keeping the low edge on the same side as the paddle sweep.

→ Exit the paddle quickly at the end of the stroke. Any hesitation will perform as a stern-rudder, turning the kayak in the opposite direction.

→ To keep up your forward momentum, follow the sweep stroke on one side with a forward stroke on the other side. If a greater turn is necessary, maintain the edge-tilt and repeat the sweep and forward combination.

Exercises

→ Practice a serpentine course around mooring buoys, floats or flotsam, taking the opportunity to travel a less than straight course. Occasionally, edge to the point of capsize to see how far you can actually tilt before losing your balance. Complete the course going forward and reverse.

→ Perform a sweep stroke and keep tilted on edge and allow the kayak to carve a gliding turn. While gliding in the turn, hold the paddle in a low-brace position with the blade just tickling the water. Edge-tilt the kayak as much as possible; your paddle is ready for a brace. It is likely that you will gain the confidence to hold a more dramatic edge-tilt.

→ RUDDER STROKES

RUDDER STROKES

When used as a rudder the paddle performs by means of its static placement in relation to the kayak and its angle of attack in relation to the water moving across the paddle. There is no significant movement or stroking of the paddle. The kayak turns around a point located along the length of the kayak usually just ahead of the seat, near to a position outboard of the paddler's mid-thigh. Placed forward or aft of this position the paddle can work to turn the kayak in either direction. The turning force generated by the paddle comes at the expense of forward momentum and excessive use of rudder-strokes to turn the kayak or keep it on course in windy conditions can result in significant loss of speed. In conditions with wind, waves or current the best choice of rudder strokes will glean some energy from the environment to assist in the turn and avoid excessive speed loss. When environmental conditions work to push the kayak off course then rudder strokes are used to turn the kayak against those effects and keep the kayak travelling on a straight course. This is particularly true of the stern-rudder stroke used to keep a steady heading on a downwind course.

Bow-rudder

Principal uses of the bow-rudder are to turn the kayak onto an up-wind course, supplement a sweep turn when making tight turns, and manoeuvring in confined spaces.

The bow-rudder is performed by placing the paddle in a static position forward of the paddler's hips. The paddle is held in a predominantly vertical orientation and placed in the water at a forward position somewhere between the paddler's hips and knees. The front face of the paddle is toward the kayak with the leading edge of the paddle rotated slightly outward, creating an angle of attack to allow the oncoming water to push against the front face of the paddle. Holding the paddle in a static position, the paddler resists the force of the water pushing on the paddle, and the bow is pulled into the turn.

The placement of the paddle responds to subtle corrections and in light winds many kayaks respond well to a paddle position only just forward of the paddler's hips. In stronger winds a slightly more forward placement will enhance the secondary effect of the wind turning the kayak. (See Turning in the wind, page 145.) In very strong winds the vertical orientation of the paddle may be hard to hold.

↑ Nic is practicing his bow rudder in calm water. Keeping his grip unchanged from a normal forward stroke he has placed the paddle in the water with the front face slightly open to the oncoming water. The lower hand has control, the upper hand is a pivot.

↑ Jen is holding her paddle out of the water to show how the bow-rudder works by orienting the blade with the correct angle of attack. The leading edge should be slightly "open" allowing the water to contact the inward (front face) of the blade. Less angle will result in less turning force, and more angle will cause excessive turbulence, ineffective turning and will slow the kayak down.

→ Be cautious when using a bow-rudder in the strongest of winds, as the non-working blade will catch the wind.

→ Edge-tilt away from the turn, there is good potential for a capsize if you edge into the direction of a bow-rudder turn.

Application

→ Use the bow-rudder when turning onto a more upwind heading (turning toward the direction of the wind).

→ Following a forward sweep stroke a bow-rudder on the other side creates a tighter turning radius.

→ A bow-draw can follow a bow-rudder to further increase a turn.

→ The bow-rudder robs you of speed and can aide in avoiding a collision by making a sudden turn and slowing down.

Key points

→ Use the bow-rudder sparingly. It turns the kayak by redirecting energy from your forward progress to a turning force, causing you to slow down.

→ Edge away from the turn-rudder stroke—the paddle works over the raised side of the kayak.

→ Lean forward slightly to assist the turn.

→ Keep a posture that will permit you to blend easily into the next stroke.

→ In light winds the working blade can be placed into the water near the paddler's knee. A more forward position is useful when turning in the wind.

→ Avoid an unnecessarily wide angle of attack with the subsequent loss of forward speed.

Exercises

→ In a moderate breeze paddle across the wind (keep the wind to your side). Make a turn upwind; use a combination of sweep, bow-rudder and forward strokes. Repeat the same turn using a sweep, stern-rudder and forward stroke. Compare the results. Don't forget to practice both left and right turns.

→ The bow-rudder is a fun stroke to play with in manoeuvring around objects or in a kelp bed. Keep up your forward speed by blending it into a forward stroke on the same side.

Stern-rudder

The stern-rudder stroke is used turn the kayak onto a downwind course, or when travelling on a downwind course to steer and compensate for effects of wind, waves or current as they push the kayak off course. The static placement of the stern-rudder is also an advantage when manoeuvring in confined spaces.

To set up for the stern-rudder, push with one foot, slightly twisting your hips and rotating your shoulders. A stern-rudder is performed with the paddle blade placed well aft of the paddler's hip. The paddle blade is near vertical and the front face is toward the kayak. The paddle shaft is positioned to create an angle of attack so that the water pushes against the back side of the paddle, pushing the stern away from the turn. Effective rudder strokes require subtle adjustments of paddle position and angle. Look in the direction you want to go—avoid looking back at the paddle when you are trying to go forward.

↑ While heading downwind, the waves overtaking from behind will often veer the kayak off course. Jen is using a stern-rudder to keep her kayak on a steady course.

↓ The swift current is pushing Michael's kayak to the right and the stern-rudder is working to turn the kayak to the left to keep the kayak on a steady course. The absence of any significant edge-tilt is purposeful; in this case edging upstream into the current might cause a capsize.

→ Rotate your upper body keeping the paddle as much in front of your chest as possible. Avoid reaching back, extending your arm and shoulder and straigtening your elbow.

Application

→ Use the stern-rudder when turning the kayak onto a new more down-wind heading (turning away from the direction of the wind).

→ When heading downwind use the stern-rudder to steer the kayak on a straight course.

→ The stern-rudder blends into a reverse sweep on the same side.

Key points

→ Rotate your upper body, keep your elbows low and near your body.

→ Edge away from the turn—rudder strokes are over the raised edge.

→ Lean back slightly to assist the turn.

Exercises

→ Find some wind and steep waves and paddle downwind. The stern-rudder will be essential in maintaining a straight line course.

→ In a moderate breeze paddle across the wind (keep the wind to your side). Make a turn downwind with a sweep and a stern-rudder. Sustain the stern-rudder and let the wind and waves push you along. Repeat the same turn using a sweep, bow-rudder combination. Compare the results. Don't forget to practice both left and right turns.

→ Find a kayaker who wants to practice their forward stroke while towing, and have them tow you. Like a water skier you can carve turns left and right with a stern-rudder.

BRACE TURNS

❻

BRACE TURNS

Brace turns are particularly useful when paddling in current or waves. A brace turn provides manoeuvrability and support at the same time. There are two concerns when trying to turn the kayak while in moving water or breaking waves. The first concern is to stay upright; the second is to perform the desired turn.

To stay upright and keep the kayak stable, the rule is to always tilt the kayak downstream. The reason for this becomes obvious if you tilt the kayak the wrong way. When the kayak is tilted correctly with the lowered edge downstream the water flows beneath the kayak and actually works in opposition to the tilt, creating a balance of forces.

If the kayak is tilted with the lower edge upstream the oncoming water piles up on deck and the subsequent capsize can be instantaneous. The upsetting effect of an upstream edge is aggravated if the paddler makes the unfortunate error of placing a brace on the upstream side of the kayak. The force of the oncoming water not only tips the kayak, it pushes the paddle under the kayak adding considerable leverage to the problem. Standing waves occur in moving water and break in an upstream direction. The paddler must brace downstream onto the face of the wave. (These are called standing waves because the wave remains in one place while the current moves past.)

In normal open water sea kayaking a right turn is made with a left edge lowered and a left sweep stroke. However, if the paddler is attempting to make this right turn while crossing an eddy line entering into a current, the left (upstream) edge and left sweep may result in a quick capsize.

The same principle is applied when the kayak is being manoeuvred while surfing on a breaking wave; without practical experience this may seem contrary. With the kayak broached on a breaking wave, the kayak is moving across a stationary body of water. The wave energy and the kayak are moving toward shore while the ocean remains stationary. The kayaker looking through a glass-bottom kayak would see the ocean going by in what appeared to be a direction heading out to sea—the kayak is moving upstream towards shore.

The consequence of all this is that the kayak must be tilted onto the crest of the wave at the same time as trying to make the kayak turn.

Low-brace turn

↑ Edging downstream allows the current to flow smoothly beneath the kayak. The paddle-brace maintains stability, and the current moving from left to right will push the bow and turn the kayak. Looking in the direction of travel, Michael's torso is rotated and his hips are able to unwind in the direction of the turn.

↑ Edging into the breaking wave and with a low-brace, Nancy is moving swiftly to her left. The water is passing under her kayak from her left to right and the raised edge of the kayak keeps her stable.

A low-brace turn is used when you need a supportive brace downstream or downwind while also making a downstream or downwind turn. A low-brace turn can produce a dramatic change of direction with a matching loss of speed. This can be good for avoiding collision with other kayakers or hidden submerged rocks.

Safety

→ Keep the leading edge of the paddle blade slightly raised so that the angle creates a lifting force, not a diving force or capsize will ensue.

Application

→ For a right turn, think lean right, brace right, turns right.

→ Low-brace turns are fun to do when speeding up to the dock or the beach. You can turn 90 degrees and come to a stop in one manoeuvre.

→ Entering a current and turning downstream.

→ Bracing on an oncoming wave and turning into the direction where the wave has come from.

Key points

→ The low-brace turn is used in conjunction with a lean into the turn. This is most appropriate when the lean and brace work to stabilize the kayak against the forces of a wave or current. Leaning into the wave or current will add stability at the same time as you perform the low-brace turn. Conversely, tilting the kayak upstream in a current or away from a steep wave will surely result in a capsize.

→ The low-brace turn is performed over the lowered edge of the kayak.

→ The bracing will slow down the forward speed of the kayak.

Exercises

→ Practice the low-brace turn as a fun manoeuvre in calm water. With good forward speed, approach a sandy beach and perform a low-brace turn just before your kayak touches the sandy bottom. You should be able to turn 90 degrees and come to a full stop without your kayak or your paddle touching bottom.

→ The same type of evasive turn can be practiced while paddling directly toward a rubber mooring buoy.

Find a location with moderate current. Starting in a calm back eddy paddle directly into the current. At the moment your feet cross the eddy line, lean downstream, rotate your body downstream and brace downstream with the paddle at or behind your seat; look where you are going (downstream), and let the current push your bow and do the work to turn the kayak.

↑ Exiting the current, the kayak is sliding to Michael's left. His high-brace both turns and supports the kayak.

High-brace turn

Safety

→ Keep the paddle in front of your chest. Your paddle blade should be easily within sight; rotate your shoulders and torso as needed if you want to place the paddle toward the stern.

Application

→ For a right turn, think lean right, brace right, turns right.

→ High-brace turns are fun to do when speeding up to the dock or the beach. You can turn 90 degrees and come to a stop in one manoeuvre.

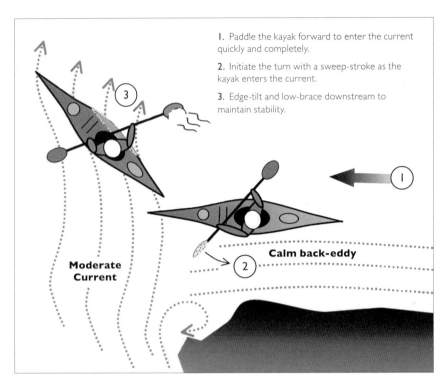

1. Paddle the kayak forward to enter the current quickly and completely.

2. Initiate the turn with a sweep-stroke as the kayak enters the current.

3. Edge-tilt and low-brace downstream to maintain stability.

Moderate Current

Calm back-eddy

↑ Eddy out, low-brace turn to cross the eddy line and continue in a downstream direction. Crossing the eddy line quickly and confidently is a principle task in keeping control of the kayak.

→ Entering a current and turning downstream.

→ Bracing on an oncoming wave and turning into the direction where the wave has come from.

Key points

→ The high-brace turn is used in conjunction with a lean into the turn. This is most appropriate when the lean and brace work to stabilize the kayak against the forces of a wave or current. Leaning into the wave or current will add stability at the same time as you perform the high-brace turn. Conversely, tilting the kayak upstream in a current or away from a steep wave will surely result in a capsize.

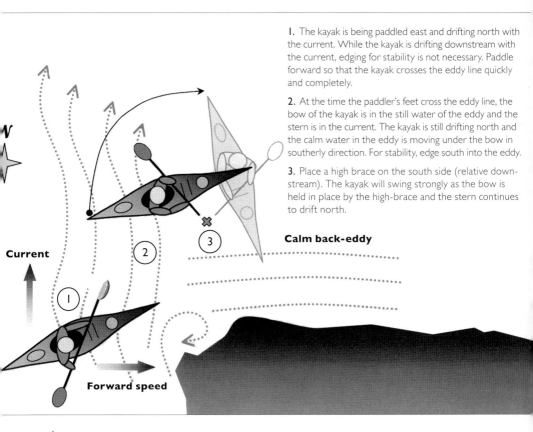

1. The kayak is being paddled east and drifting north with the current. While the kayak is drifting downstream with the current, edging for stability is not necessary. Paddle forward so that the kayak crosses the eddy line quickly and completely.

2. At the time the paddler's feet cross the eddy line, the bow of the kayak is in the still water of the eddy and the stern is in the current. The kayak is still drifting north and the calm water in the eddy is moving under the bow in southerly direction. For stability, edge south into the eddy.

3. Place a high brace on the south side (relative downstream). The kayak will swing strongly as the bow is held in place by the high-brace and the stern continues to drift north.

Calm back-eddy

Current

Forward speed

↑ Eddy in, high-brace turn to cross the eddy line and stop in the calm water. As the kayak enters the eddy the effective current is from the kayaker's left to right.

→ The high-brace turn is performed over the lowered edge of the kayak.

→ The bracing will slow down the forward speed of the kayak.

Exercises

→ With a small wave approaching from the right side, paddle forward and lean slightly right toward the wave, and place a high-brace on the right side in a forward position near your knees. The paddle should turn the bow to the right while the passing wave pushes the stern left aiding in the turn. Blend the high-brace into a forward stroke and continue to paddle out in the direction from where the wave came from.

→ A similar application of the high-brace turn is to exit a current into a calm eddy.

DRAW STROKES

DRAW STROKES

Draw strokes are used to move the kayak sideways. Lateral movement is necessary for approaching a partner's kayak from the side or manoeuvring near to a dock. During aid or rescue situations it is often necessary to move the kayak laterally, quickly manoeuvring into a position ready to give assistance. While underway a draw stroke can be used to avoid an obstacle at the same time as keeping a steady heading moving forward.

There can be some confusion around the names of various draw strokes. Three draw strokes are outlined below along with other strokes closely related to each of these three.

A standard draw is performed when the kayak is stationary. The paddle is placed in a near-vertical position outboard of the paddler's hip and pulled in directly toward the side of the kayak, causing the kayak to move sideways. The standard draw can be repeated in a reciprocal in-and-out motion with only the inward stroke generating the drawing action.

The sculling draw, like the standard draw, is performed when the kayak is stationary. The paddle is placed in the same general position as in the standard draw but the paddle is stroked forward and backward, relative to the kayak. The drawing action is generated by the angle of attack alternating with each change of direction. The sculling draw can be performed in a continuous manner.

The hanging draw occurs when the kayak is moving forward. The paddle is held stationary as the water flows over the paddle blade. The paddle is held with an angle of attack so that the flow of water over the blade pulls the kayak sideways toward the paddle. The drawing action can continue only as long as there is water passing over the paddle blade.

VARIATIONS ON THE THEME OF A DRAW STROKE

The point of paddling is to have control over your kayak and move it in the direction of your choice. Practicing individually named strokes in isolation is like doing drills and exercises during a soccer practice; by themselves the drills and exercises can be fun and useful but the intention is to have a mastery of skills suitable for the spontaneity of game day. In some cases the name of an individual stroke refers to motion of the paddle, as in the forward and backward motion of the sculling draw or the in-and-out reciprocating action of the standard draw. In other cases the name of the stroke refers to the static placement of the paddle, as in the mid-ships position for the hanging draw (for moving the kayak sideways) and the more forward position of the paddle for the bow-rudder (for turning the kayak). Change the position of the hanging draw to a more forward position and it becomes a bow-rudder; move the hanging draw aft and it becomes a stern-rudder. If you move the otherwise static bow-rudder laterally inward toward the kayak that action would be called a bow draw. Similarly a stern-rudder can easily turn into a stern-draw.

Standard draw

With an upright posture and the upper torso rotated toward the side the paddle is planted, turn the front face of the paddle toward you and fully submerge it in a position out from the kayak and in line of the hips. Keep your normal grip on the paddle shaft. The lower arm is extended with the elbow slightly bent. The upper forearm is near horizontal and the upper hand reaches near to or over the deck seam. The upper hand takes a light grip and a static position providing a fulcrum for the movement of the paddle. Plant the paddle deep, well out from the side of the kayak with the lower hand very close to the water.

Throughout the stroke the paddle shaft should be as near to vertical as possible. The upper hand remains almost static. Draw the paddle directly inward toward the kayak. Stop the draw stroke before the paddle shaft contacts the kayak. To repeat the stroke, leave the paddle in the water and cock your lower wrist to turn the paddle blade 90 degrees and slice it back out to the starting position. Reposition it for a second stroke. Keep the blade submerged throughout both the inward and outward phase of the stroke and repeat the stroke as many times as required. Only the inward portion of the stroke produces a drawing action.

↑ A standard draw stroke has the leading edge up. With the blade deep, the water is pushed beneath the hull.

↑ James prefers to edge in toward the draw stroke. It gives him greater reach and power, but the kayak will push more water.

↑ Keep the paddle slightly out from the side of the kayak. A common error is to draw the paddle too close to the kayak. As Ian's kayak travels to his right, it can push against the paddle causing the blade to go under the hull and he might just capsize.

↑ With the paddle placed in a forward position and drawing the paddle in diagonally to her hip, Jen will move the kayak forward and to the side.

A deep paddle placement efficiently pushes the water beneath the hull. Power is lost with too shallow a placement as water is pushed against the side of the kayak. As the kayak draws sideways the kayak can be edge-tilted upward on the leading edge allowing the hull to slide smoothly across the water. This can be particularly important in a current or steep wave. Edging in the opposite direction causes the submerged edge to plow into the water and is generally not preferred. However, I have seen skilled paddlers tilt down toward their draw stroke and take advantage of the extra reach gained by leaning out into the stroke.

The kayak is prone to capsizing if the paddle comes very close or collides with the side of the kayak. There is a tendency for this to happen when the direction of travel is with the wind and the kayak is drifting sideways with the stroke. The momentum of the kayak can push the kayak over the paddle and capsize. End the draw stroke with the paddle a short distance away from the kayak.

BOW AND STERN DRAW, VARIATIONS ON A STANDARD DRAW

The standard draw is sometimes renamed depending on the initial position of the paddle. As described above, if you plant the paddle directly away from your hip and draw it in toward your hip the kayak will move sideways. A bow draw has the paddle planted in a position farther forward near your knees. Consequently, the bow of the kayak will move toward the paddle and the bow will move sideways and turn toward the paddle. A stern draw has the paddle planted in a position behind your hips, and drawing the paddle in will cause the stern of the kayak to move toward the paddle. In the case of the stern draw, the heading of the kayak will turn away from the paddle. When coming up along side another boat or a dock, the bow and stern draws are used to keep the kayak parallel to the boat or dock. The bow draw is often used as a subtle supplement to other turning strokes such as the bow-rudder.

Sculling draw

The sculling draw uses a continuous forward and backward (relative to the bow and stern of the kayak) alternating stroke to pull the kayak sideways in a steady motion. The sculling draw starts with the paddle planted in the same position as for the standard draw, outboard of the kayak approximately in line with the paddler's hip. The torso is well turned and the paddle is in a near vertical position with both hands reaching over the edge of the kayak. (See Standard Draw, above.)

The paddle is stroked alternately forward and backward. The front face of the paddle must have a slightly open angle of attack. This creates a drawing force as the paddle is stroked each way. As the stroke alternates and the direction changes, so must the angle of the paddle. The stroke can be performed with action of the arms alone. For additional power, alternating torso twisting puts larger muscle groups into action.

SCULLING HIGH-BRACE, VARIATIONS ON A SCULLING DRAW

If the angle of the paddle shaft is moved to a more horizontal position, the sculling provides more support than lateral drawing motion and the stroke is then called a sculling high-brace. (See Sculling high-brace, page 57.)

Hanging draw

With the kayak moving forward, a hanging draw moves the kayak sideways. This stroke is done to avoid obstacles or come alongside another moving kayak or a stationary dock. Like a rudder stroke, the hanging draw involves planting the paddle without any stroking motion. Planting the paddle somewhere between a bow-rudder and stern-rudder will cause the kayak to move sideways without turning; this is the placement for the hanging draw.

It is often the case that the hanging draw, while moving the kayak sideways, will also cause the kayak to turn toward the side of the stroke. (A right-side draw stroke tends to turn the kayak to the right.) This is caused by the paddle being placed in a position too far forward. To draw the kayak directly sideways without any turning, the paddler must rotate their shoulders fully to the direction of the hanging draw. Pushing with the working-side leg and slipping in the seat, while rotating the hips, will help get the maximum of torso rotation. Edge-tilting the kayak slightly down on the side of the stroke will help to further counteract the turning effect.

↑ Often obstacles are not as obvious as this one and you can avoid the collision by drawing the kayak sideways with a hanging draw stroke.

↑ With the paddle placed in the water and the leading edge open to the current, the kayak will be drawn sideways away from the obstacle.

BOW- AND STERN-RUDDER, VARIATIONS ON A HANGING DRAW

A hanging draw is when the kayak is moving forward and the paddle is placed near the paddler's hip to move the kayak sideways. If the paddle position is moved forward the kayak will turn toward the paddle. This is called a bow-rudder. Similarly, if the paddle is planted aft the kayak will turn away from the paddle and this stroke is called a stern-rudder.

Safety

→ The working blade must be kept a small distance away from the side of the kayak. As the kayak moves sideways the working blade of the paddle can be driven under the kayak and a capsize is likely.

Application

→ Moving sideways to assist a paddling partner.

→ A hanging draw can be used to avoid obstacles while maintaining a steady heading.

→ Close-in manoeuvring alongside a boat or dock.

→ At times it is useful to paddle in such a manner as to stay in one place and keep a steady heading. Bow- and stern-draws help to compensate for the turning effects of wind and waves.

Key points

→ The paddle should be placed deep and fully immersed. At the end of the stroke the wash from the paddle should be directed beneath the kayak.

→ To draw the kayak laterally, without any forward or backward progress, the paddle is placed in a position approximately in line with the hip.

→ The upper torso is turned in the direction of travel—look where you are going.

→ Use body rotation to add power.

→ The sculling draw is done with smooth and steady strokes.

Exercises

→ With a paddling partner orient two kayaks bow to bow with about 1 m between the bows. The two paddlers simultaneously draw stroke to move their kayaks sideways in the same direction. Throughout the drawing action the kayaks should stay 1 m apart, directly in line with each other. This exercise teaches control of speed, direction of motion and turning. This exercise provides ample feedback showing the paddlers the end result of their draw strokes.

→ Come together: While paddling forward it is common for two kayaks to meander too close together and paddles begin to interfere with each other. To separate the two kayaks while underway each paddler should perform one hanging draw stroke. The exercise can be repeated as the paddlers move forward and manoeuvre their kayaks close together and apart again.

→ Sideways race: With two kayaks side by side, 2 m apart, the paddlers begin to draw stroke in the same direction. One paddler tries to catch up to the other in a short race.

ROLLING

8

ROLLING

Does rolling belong in a short book on sea kayak strokes or should it be reserved for a discussion of rescues? The process of learning to roll greatly improves edge control, brace turns, recovery braces and overall confidence. Just trying to learn to roll improves general paddling skill and increases your confidence and safety. An introduction to rolling in calm water is included here as a fundamental paddling skill; it is an elemental part of learning efficient kayak strokes.

The first quarter of a roll requires no practice at all; gravity will do the work. The second and third quarters require you to be calm and patient. Leaning forward as close as possible to the deck helps let the kayak roll around to the other side. The last quarter of the roll is essentially a high-brace. The key elements to learn are confidence, timing and enough practice to train your body to accurately and reliably perform a sequence of movements. In a full roll the paddler's buttocks pass overhead; for most people this not a usual posture and will disorient most new paddlers. To alleviate this disorientation it is helpful to first learn a half-roll where the capsize and recovery are on the same side. This is called a half-roll, and your buttocks do not pass over your head.

Rolling a kayak in calm water is very easy to do, but learning to do it takes some time and persistence, and the learning is more fun and much quicker with the aid of a good coach.

Coaching and practicing

Comfortable progress in learning to roll involves learning the component parts of a roll in reverse order, from the end result backward to the starting position. Learning to roll involves being relaxed and getting it right a few times so that your body can experience the correct motions. Critical in this process is to practice good technique and success at each point along the way.

Before getting into your kayak you can practice some of the correct motions for rolling.

KAYAK SIT-UPS

Sit on the ground as if in a kayak, with your legs bent out ahead of you and your torso upright. Cross your arms over your chest and keep them there throughout the exercise. Lean well forward and capsize gently over onto the grass, then return to an upright sitting position. You may not use or move your arms. To recover to a sitting position it is easy to stretch out, layback, roll onto your back and then sit up—success. This is what I call a kayak sit-up. Do not use your hands or elbows for any assistance. Perform the kayak sit-up in a smooth, continuous motion. If someone supports your feet and knees this is even easier.

Try to repeat the exercise but this time, you may not lean forward, you may not lie back (keep that 90 degree angle between your torso and legs), and no one may hold your feet and knees. As before, keep your arms folded on your chest. Capsizing is swift and painful. You will find it is not possible to sit up when lifting your head while still bent 90 degrees at the waist; the same is true on the water. In the case of a roll or brace, bring your head up last.

Repeat a few kayak sit-ups, keeping each motion well defined and with smooth graceful transitions: lean forward, capsize, and lay back extending your body, roll onto your back and then sit up. Note that the upper body travels in a generally circular motion as the muscle groups in your stomach and back are engaged to get you upright. The head also moves in a generally circular motion around the neck: tilted forward, down to the side, then tilted back before sitting upright. Some repeated practice will ingrain this sequence of actions in your mind and your muscles. The kayak sit-up is easier to do if someone holds your feet and knees. You can engage the muscles of your legs and lower torso when your legs are supported.

In your kayak, tilting and recovering is much easier if your cockpit fits you well and you can get support in the kayak with your feet, knees and hips.

This first exercise on land usually translates easily to practice on the water but a swimmer's nose-plug may be a welcome comfort aid.

HIPPY-HIPPY SHAKE

The hip-flick is a body motion that all skilled paddlers have automated into their nervous system. (See the diagram of the hip-flick on page 44.) Sit in the kayak, relax and gently tilt your head left and right—like a bobble-head doll. The sides of the kayak will tilt up right and left. Accentuate this motion with a little tilting of the hips. The correct motion is natural and intuitive; the direction of the head motion is in opposition to the direction of the hip motion. Remember that in the kayak the leg on the rising side of the kayak is the knee principally involved in doing the work. Alternately repeat the hippy-hippy shake and think of gently kneeing yourself in one ear and then the other—gently now.

This motion will warm up your spine and hips for the hip-flick and get you used to keeping your head low. A few kayak sit-ups and then the hippy-hippy shake will get you warmed up, relaxed and flexible.

First exercise

With a paddle float slipped over the blade take an extended grip and place the paddle on the water as in a high-brace (right-hand side). Relax, lay back and look up. Swing your shoulders a little sideways to the right into the water; trying to get both shoulders and your back onto the surface of the water. Have as much of your PFD as possible contacting the water.

↑ Hippy shake

Relax and keep looking up—rotate your body and try to get your left shoulder into the water while looking at the sky. Recovering from this position is the last part of a roll. Just like on the grass, look up to the sky, move sideways from being in the water at the side of the kayak to a layback position over the aft deck, and then sit up. See photo on the next page.

Second exercise

Perform a gentle capsize to your right. With the paddle extended, place the blade with the paddle float attached on the right-hand edge of the kayak. Tilt the kayak and lean just enough to approach a capsize. Before it actually does capsize do a high-brace to bring yourself upright again on an even keel. Head tilts towards the water, hips are loose, hip-flick.

↑ Exercise 1

Third exercise

With the working paddle on the left-hand deck seam tilt the kayak until you capsize to the right. Sweep the paddle from its resting position onto the water and high-brace for recovery. Keep your elbows low and near your body.

Fourth exercise—half-roll

Set up with the paddle on the left-hand deck seam and capsize to the right. Do not move your paddle from its position resting on the left-hand deck seam. Capsize with a big splash and pause for a moment; you will submerge a little before your PFD and the paddle float raise you to the surface. When the splashing comes to an end, sweep the paddle and

↑ Exercise 2

↓ Exercise 3

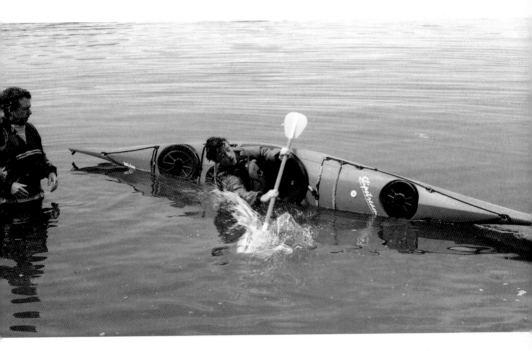

↑ Gain confidence and good technique with several small capsizes and braces done correctly before moving onto more dramatic capsizes.

high-brace for recovery. When you capsize to the right and high-brace right for recovery, the move is called a half-roll.

Fifth exercise—full roll

Set up as for exercise #4, then capsize fully to your LEFT. Wait a second and your buttocks will go over your head and everything will seem reversed, but it is all the same as before. After staying tucked and holding your breath you are in a position to sweep, brace and recover on the RIGHT, just as you did before. This, of course, is a full roll.

During the full capsize and roll, the beginner usually gets disoriented. Without someone to restrain their confused efforts, they try to brace up on the wrong side and the muscle memories of the previous practice are quickly confused and erased. To ensure that the paddle can only be swept out in the correct direction the training partner or instructor should use a line attached to the paddle float.

Important tip: When the paddler is set in the position to capsize, the line on the paddle float must lead from the upper edge of the float. As the student makes the sweep, the partner can put a light tension on the line to raise the leading edge of the paddle and keep the paddle sweeping near the surface of the water.

If problems and errors occur, as they often do, go all the way back to the first exercise for a couple repetitions and work through the sequence. While training those muscles, try to remember the correct motions.

ROLLING THE KAYAK

Set up on the left-hand side, tuck your head low closely toward your left knee and capsize to the left. Stay tucked low until you have rolled three-quarters of the way around and arrive on the right-hand side where you have been practicing all along. After almost one sideways revolution most beginners are quite disoriented and although the motions required to roll up are exactly what you have already practiced, it all feels very different. I would not suggest struggling on your own. At this point if you can have a few successful rolls with some help you will be well on your way to rolling the kayak on your own.

When you are happy with your progress cut one-third off the end of your homemade inexpensive paddle float and repeat. As in the past, if you encounter problems, put the cut-off piece of the float back on and practice getting it right. If a two-thirds paddle float is sufficient, take it off and use the one-third-size piece. Soon you will roll without the aide of the paddle float.

↑ Preparing for a full roll.

↑ Capsize to the left.

↓ Just a little tension on the string is usually enough to keep the paddle on the surface and assure a successful practice roll. Roll up on the right.

Safety

→ Practice with a competent and trusted friend nearby to lend a hand.

→ Check that the spray skirt is easily removed.

→ Keep your elbows in near your body.

→ Avoid excessive effort; rolling does not require any exertion. Frantic attempts to "make it work" can lead to sore or injured shoulders.

→ Rolling can be hard on the lower back. Warm up and avoid too many repetitions.

Application

→ The process of learning to roll improves general paddling skill and increases your confidence and safety.

→ Rolling is a significant defence against turning a simple capsize into a complicated rescue.

Key points

→ Repeated small success.

→ Work backwards so that your body learns the target behaviour.

→ Use a training aid for repeated practice, and avoid struggling to get it right.

→ Reduce the reliance on the training aid.

Exercises

Failed rolls are often 50 percent successful. The paddler reaches the surface in an unstable position. Rather than submerging to set up for another roll, the paddler has the alternative of sculling for support and then executing a high-brace. As a follow-up to a partially successful roll, this technique has the advantage of offering the opportunity for a breath of air, although taking a breath while still unstable takes good timing and a cool head. In controlled conditions, you can practice rolling left and right, feigning an unsuccessful first effort, then setting up for a second effort. When your roll is not working successfully, make it a rule to attempt rolling at least three times before you choose to pull off your spray skirt and exit the kayak; learn to relax and persist.

BLENDED STROKES

9

BLENDED STROKES

An Irish sea kayaker and coach once told me, "Paddling is like a good Irish Stew. The strokes are the meat, potatoes, carrots and onions, but a good stew is so much more than its ingredients; it takes time to simmer and make the gravy—and ohh...a good stew is all about dipping into the gravy."

There is a great deal of individual choice in how a paddler might combine and blend strokes together. Each wave and each heading demand a creative response from the paddler. Here are a few typical blended strokes that will work in specific circumstances.

Combined strokes for turning:
→ Forward—sweep—bow-rudder—forward.
→ Forward—sweep—stern-rudder—forward.

For turning, combining a sweep stroke with a bow-rudder or a sweep with a stern-rudder uses both the left and right paddle blades to turn in the same direction. The timing between blended strokes is an important consideration. It takes less effort to keep the kayak moving forward than it does to pick up lost speed, and a quick linking of blended strokes is better at controlling and maintaining a good rate of speed. It is important to keep in mind that a sweep stroke adds to forward momentum while a rudder stroke reduces forward momentum.

To turn to the right, sweep the left paddle through the water and follow that stroke immediately by a bow-rudder stroke on the right-hand side. The left sweep stroke concludes with the right paddle in a forward position ready for a right bow-rudder stroke. Rudder strokes work by the proper placement of the paddle without any stroking of the paddle through the water. The bow-rudder is placed forward of the paddler's hips with the front side of the paddle facing forward. The front face of the paddle pushes against the oncoming water. The bow-rudder on the right-hand side blends easily into a forward stroke on the same side making for a smooth and effective combination of left sweep, right bow-rudder and right forward stroke.

A similar combination for the same right turn is to sweep on the left and place a stern-rudder stroke on the right-hand side. After the sweep is complete, this combination requires that the paddler swing the right paddle aft to a position near the stern. The stern-rudder on the right is followed by the next forward stroke on the left. Place the stern-rudder stroke well aft of the paddler's hips with the front face of the paddle toward the kayak. The back face of the paddle pushes against the oncoming water. The effectiveness of a rudder stroke depends on the proper paddle placement, paddle angle and the kayak having good forward speed.

PADDLING TECHNIQUES FOR WIND

Much of our sea kayaking is done when the weather and the sea conditions are fine. Many of us paddle for several seasons and never encounter the conditions that would demand the maximum of our skills. The impression we get is that we are doing just fine and our skills are more than good enough, until an unexpected change of weather or an error in judgment has us paddling frantically, anxious to get ashore. To prepare ourselves for the rougher-than-planned day we need to practice the very best technique on the gentle days. To test our technique, we need to get out and practice on a few of the rougher days.

↑ It pays big dividends to paddle efficiently while travelling upwind.

PREFERRED HEADING (WEATHERCOCKING)

Consider the kayak's behaviour without using a rudder or skeg. As the kayak moves forward through the water, the bow and stern encounter different forces. The bow moves forward into undisturbed water pushing it aside. At the stern, the water moves in to fill the void created by the passage of the middle of the kayak leaving a turbulent wake in the kayak's path. In calm air these forces are balanced on both sides of the kayak. But if the wind is blowing and pushing the kayak at all sideways the difference between the forces at the bow and stern will often result in weathercocking. Pushed sideways, the bow meets the resistance of the undisturbed water being pushed aside. The stern meets the weaker resistance of the water as it moves in to fill in the void created by the passage of the middle of the kayak. In the undisturbed water the bow has higher "lateral resistance" and it is pushed downwind a relatively small amount. In the more turbulent water the lateral resistance is lower at the stern, and it is pushed downwind more than the bow. From the paddler's perspective the bow is pulled up into the wind. As the paddling speed increases, the fore and aft difference in lateral resistance grows and the kayak veers increasingly upwind.

Choosing your strokes to work in concert with the forces imparted by the wind and the motion of the kayak will improve your performance. Turning the kayak in the wind begins with good forward speed and using the paddle effectively on both sides of the kayak. Having a cockpit seat and foot braces that fit your body helps transmit the efforts of all your strokes to your kayak. For turning in the wind you will need good basic skills with the sweep stroke and the rudder strokes.

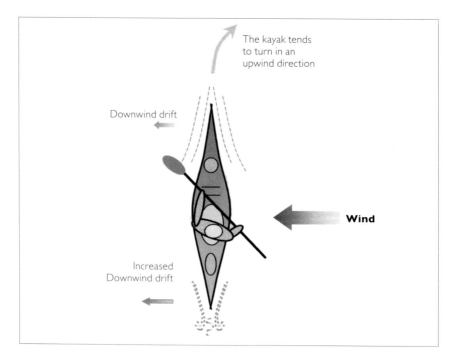

The kayak tends to turn in an upwind direction

Downwind drift

Wind

Increased Downwind drift

↑ As the kayak moves forward, the resistance of the water around the kayak changes and the effects of the wind will change. Turbulence at the stern creates a region of less resistance and downwind drift increases. The kayak tends to turn in an up-wind direction, this tendency is called weathercocking.

Paddling upwind

Paddling upwind is about having an efficient forward paddling technique, ample power and endurance. Most kayaks will track into the wind, and keeping a steady heading is easy. The paddler's job is to move the kayak forward, putting shoulder and back into a good stroke. It is generally more effective to paddle more frequently, maintaining a higher cadence, than it is to put more effort into each stroke. Like walking uphill with a pack on your back, it is better to take more short strides than take fewer long strides. Faced with an energy-intense task, it is important to have efficient paddling technique that wastes as little energy as possible. That technique must also suit the human body's ability to deliver power to each stroke. Power consumes energy and the body has a limited capacity to replenish energy reserves. Good paddling technique works in conjunction with the body's ability to regenerate. An efficient forward paddling stroke uses energy only slightly faster than the body can regenerate it. We need to arrive at our destination before energy reserves are exhausted.

Making good speed against the wind has definite advantages. You will expend less energy if you minimize the time spent fighting the wind; get ashore and out of the wind before it blows any harder or you run out of energy. Arriving at your final destination on time is more than convenient. Navigational plans may have included critical times to avoid tidal currents or daily thermal winds. When navigating by dead reckoning the accuracy of distance estimates decreases with more time spent on the water. Longer time spent trying to keep a compass course can result in greater errors.

Paddling downwind

Paddling downwind is more about directional control than it is about forward power. Waves overtaking you from behind push the stern of the kayak ahead but the bow encounters the relatively still water found on the back side of the wave. As a consequence the stern wants to accelerate faster than the bow and the kayak tends to turn off course. Sailors will say that the boat yaws. If the overtaking wave is large and steep the boat will turn fully sideways to the wave. This is called broaching. When travelling downwind, rudders and skegs are very helpful for keeping the kayak on a steady course. Efficient paddling on a downwind course requires anticipating the turning effects of an overtaking wave as well as the effective use of edging and a stern-rudder.

Turning in the wind

In calm conditions a sweep stroke is usually sufficient to turn the kayak, but when the wind blows, turning the kayak may require more than a sweep stroke alone. Depending on the relative direction of the wind and the direction you want to turn, some strokes will work more effectively than others, and you can let the wind do some of the work for you. In choosing which strokes to use, it is helpful to understand how the forces imparted by the wind and the water affect the directional control of the kayak.

TURNING RIGHT TO A MORE UPWIND HEADING

An effective choice for turning a kayak right to a more upwind heading is to start with good forward speed, look right, edge-tilt left and sweep on the left (downwind) side. While maintaining the left (downwind) edge-tilt, follow the sweep with a bow-rudder on the right (upwind) side. It's best not to rush the sweep then make a quick transition to the bow-rudder.

During the bow-rudder, the paddle's angle of attack will pull the bow to the right and its forward placement will increase the lateral resistance at the bow, retarding the bow's downwind drift while the stern remains free to drift, complementing the turn. Hold the bow-rudder for only a moment to avoid any significant loss of speed. A loss of speed is detrimental to an upwind turn because it decreases weathercocking, making it difficult to regain speed against the wind. To help maintain your speed, blend the bow-rudder stroke into a forward stroke on the same side. Be sure to keep the forward stroke straight back so it doesn't become a sweep stroke, turning you in the wrong direction.

For upwind turns a bow-rudder is an effective tool, but strokes with an aft paddle placement have a distinct disadvantage. It is quite common for beginners to use a stern-rudder when trying to turn the kayak upwind. Some will even revert to a reverse sweep when they discover the stern-rudder doesn't work. To make matters worse, a reverse sweep dramatically slows down any remaining forward speed.

TURNING LEFT TO A MORE DOWNWIND HEADING

To turn a kayak left to a more downwind heading start with good forward speed, look left (downwind), edge-tilt right (upwind) and sweep on the right (upwind) side. While maintaining the right (upwind) edge-tilt, follow the sweep with a stern-rudder on the left (downwind) side. Don't rush the sweep, but finish off with a quick transition to the stern-rudder.

During the stern-rudder, the paddle's angle of attack against the on-coming water will initiate the turn and the aft placement of the paddle in the water will retard the downwind drift of the stern while allowing the bow to freely drift downwind, aiding the turn. You can hold the stern-rudder for a moment; a small loss of speed reduces weathercocking and is easily regained downwind with one or two forward strokes.

KEEPING A STEADY COURSE IN THE WIND

On a blustery day, with the kayak already travelling on the desired heading, your kayak will naturally waver and wander. Techniques for correcting a wavering course are much the same as turning onto a new heading, but the emphasis will vary.

For small corrections on an upwind heading avoid the bow-rudder stroke because it reduces overall speed. To make a small right (upwind) course correction, anticipate by looking and twisting your upper torso in the direction you are intending to turn, edge-tilt left (downwind) and

↑ The bow-rudder turns the kayak towards the blade and allows the stern to drift downwind. Continue with forward strokes to keep the kayak moving forward.

sweep on the left (downwind) side. Concentrating on untwisting your lower torso will help the kayak ease back onto course. At the end of a sweep stroke remember to lift the paddle out of the water quickly so that it does not act as a contrary stern-rudder stroke. To make a small left (downwind) course correction, edge-tilt right (upwind) and sweep on the right (upwind) side. As always look where you are going and untwist your lower torso. If the wind is at your back pushing you forward, follow the sweep with a left (downwind) stern-rudder.

↑ The stern-rudder turns the kayak towards the blade and allows the bow to drift downwind (on a downwind heading). Any loss of speed from using a stern-rudder is easily regained.

Effective paddling in dynamic sea conditions requires the ability to adapt and blend turning strokes to suit specific circumstances. Knowing how to use the paddle to work in concert with the wind and waves will get you where you want to go.

TURNING IN WAVES

Turning strokes are most effective when timed to coincide with the best position on a passing wave. As a wave passes it can lift the bow or the stern of the kayak partially out of the water. Turn upwind when the bow and your bow-rudder are in the water and the stern is lifted free to drift downwind. A downwind turn works best when the stern and your stern-rudder are in the water and the bow is lifted free to drift downwind. When the wave is steep and its crest is breaking, your concerns for stability will take precedence over turning. You would likely capsize if you tried to do a right (upwind) turn with the usual sweep stroke on the left (downwind) with the kayak edged left (downwind) away from the oncoming wave crest. In this case, to remain upright and stable, it is necessary to edge into an oncoming breaking wave, regardless of the direction of an intended turn. A right (upwind) turn in steep waves can be accomplished with a high-brace turn. The kayak is edged right into the wave and the paddle is placed as a high-brace in a forward position. (Lean forward to set the brace and keep your elbows close to your sides.) The edge and brace adds considerable stability, and the forward paddle placement holds the bow steady against the wind while the forces of the wind and the oncoming wave will turn the kayak by pushing the stern downwind and down-wave. A high-brace turn can significantly reduce forward speed especially with the added opposition of an oncoming breaking wave. After the wave

↓ Turning is easier when a wave lifts the bow and stern out of the water.

passes you must paddle forward vigorously to keep up good speed and maintain your new heading.

To make a right turn downwind in steep waves it is still necessary to maintain stability by edging into the oncoming wave. While maintaining your commitment to stability and edging into the wave, turn your upper body to look where you are going and with some care, place the paddle for a stern-rudder. The wave will push your bow downwind, turning the kayak while the stern-rudder paddle position will hold the stern from drifting. Stability relies on a sustained commitment to edging into the wave and any lack of commitment to edging here will surely cause a capsize. In steep seas a downwind turn, even off a small wave, is one of sea kayaking's more demanding manoeuvres. Practice in deep water where you can roll or exit and swim as might be necessary.

Turning a loaded sea kayak in the wind and waves can be a daunting task. A forward sweep is a preferred turning stroke because it preserves forward speed. With the addition of an outward tilt the kayak tracks an arc in the desired direction noticeably improving the turn. Edge left, sweep out to the left, and the kayak will make a good right turn. To continue turning and maintain good forward speed, keep the kayak on edge, follow the sweep stroke on the left with a forward stroke on the right and once again sweep on the left. Keep the kayak tilted for as long as you want to continue the turn. When the kayak is no longer tilted, it will once again track in a straight line.

For a leaned turn, the kayak must be moving forward at good speed. Start the turn with a reverse sweep stroke and tilt the kayak strongly by leaning out over the side of the kayak, committing to the support of a paddle-brace. The angle of the paddle makes a transition from vertical at the start of the sweep to horizontal for the brace. Lean right, reverse sweep right, and the kayak will make a sharp right turn. A leaned turn can turn the kayak through 90 degrees with only one stroke, but at the cost of a significant loss of forward speed. However, aggressive leaned turns are used in situations such as turning seaward to exit a surf wave or turning upwind to exit a steep breaking wind wave, where losing speed is less important than maintaining stability. Note that a leaned turn has the kayak tilted inwards toward the turn.

In the steep waves of a tide rip or the larger breakers of a beach, tilting the kayak is necessary to remain stable and upright. When waves get steep enough, they can force a kayak to turn sideways to the wave. As a surf wave or a wind wave causes a kayak to broach, the paddler must edge the kayak into the advancing wave to maintain stability. When the kayak is broached and surfing sideways, raise the leading edge to slide across the water. Edging may be adequate for small waves, but when you are faced with a large steep wave, an aggressive lean toward the wave and a high-brace set deep into the wave may be necessary to counter the considerable forces that would capsize the kayak. The technique used to lean and brace into a breaking wind wave is the same as you would use with a standing wave formed by moving water, as in the case of an overfall. The paddler moving with the current, toward the wave, needs to edge (or lean) and brace onto the wave. Be assured that edging or leaning the wrong way in any breaking wave will result in a sudden and forceful capsize.

PADDLING IN CURRENT

Current has several characteristics that are of interest to sea kayakers. Current travelling over an irregular shallow sea floor alters the surface shape of the water producing standing waves, boils, upwelling and whirlpools. For the most part, sea kayakers can skirt around moving water hazards but even the most cautious paddler must eventually submit to paddling through a tide rip. The natural environment that the sea kayaker inhabits is too dynamic and chaotic to permit perfect predictions. Plans must allow for wide margin for variability. Capable paddlers have the skills in reserve for unexpected bad sea conditions. Learning to judge the effects of moving water while paddling a sea kayak is a challenge with significant demands and considerable rewards.

↑ Experience paddling in current is an excellent way to practice and improve technical paddling skills.

The coastal sea kayaker will encounter chaotic water that includes wind waves, reflected waves and standing waves, sometimes all at once. While the expert surf kayaker or white water rodeo paddler are masters of angle, motion, tilt and timing, the touring sea kayaker needs to know the fundamentals. A 5.5-metre-long loaded sea kayak is not designed to do tricks but a sea kayaker with a few tricks up their sleeve will get safely through waves and current.

APPENDIX

BOOKS BY THE AUTHOR

→ *Savvy Paddler*

→ *Handbook of Safety and Rescue*

→ *Sea Kayak Around Vancouver Island*

THE FOLLOWING NATIONAL ASSOCIATIONS CAN PROVIDE A WEALTH OF INFORMATION.

→ Paddle Canada ... www.paddlingcanada.com

→ American Canoe & Kayak Association ... www.acanet.org

→ British Canoe Union (USA) ... www.bcuna.com

→ British Canoe Union (UK) ... www.bcu.org.uk

In your area inquire about sea kayak guiding associations, provincial and regional paddling associations and local clubs. Local clubs have a wealth of information and resources and their members can advise you on where to find the commercial outfitters that provide the services and products you are looking for.

ABOUT THE AUTHOR

A leader at the national level, Doug Alderson has been a contributing member of Paddle Canada (formerly CRCA) since the inception of the national sea kayaking program. Formerly a Coach-3 in the British Canoe Union system, he is currently chairman of Paddle Canada's Sea Kayak Program Development Committee. As a senior instructor trainer, Alderson is responsible for training paddlers and certifying instructors at all levels from sea to sea to sea. He is the author of three other kayaking books, including *Sea Kayak Around Vancouver Island* (Rocky Mountain Books).

ON THE WATER...
WITH **ROCKY MOUNTAIN BOOKS**

• Sea Kayak Around Vancouver Island
Doug Alderson

ISBN 1-894765-50-8 | $16.95, softcover

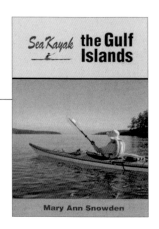

Sea Kayak the Gulf Islands •
Mary Ann Snowden

ISBN 1-894765-51-6 | $16.95, softcover

• Sea Kayak Nootka & Kyuquot Sounds
Heather Harbord

ISBN 1-894765-52-4 | $16.95, softcover

Visit rmbooks.com for more great outdoor books

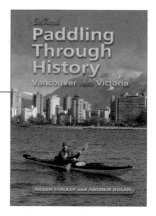

Sea Kayak Paddling Through •
History: Vancouver and Victoria
Aileen Stalker and Andrew Nolan

ISBN 1-894765-57-5 | $19.95, softcover

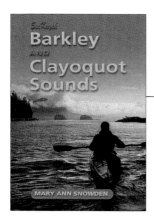

Sea Kayak Barkley
and Clayoquot Sounds
Mary Ann Snowden

ISBN 1-894765-54-0 | $19.95, softcover

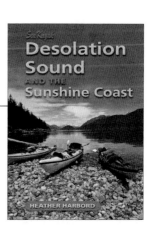

Sea Kayak Desolation Sound •
and the Sunshine Coast
Heather Harbord

ISBN 1-894765-53-2 | $19.95, softcover